Keto Holiday Table: The

Brunch & Appetizers

Main Meals & Sides

Desserts & Drinks

Happy Holidays!

More than any other time of year, we find these winter holidays bring up memories and traditions we were raised with. As we grew up, our families grew, and we found new food traditions folding into our lives.

Those food memories didn't evaporate just because we moved towards living lives on the Proper Human Diet.

We incorporated our favorites into our plans, and in some cases made some substitutions in our recipes so that we could continue to enjoy them while enjoying good health!

Because these are unique occasion recipes, we aren't including macros nor do we require these recipes to be 0 carbs, though some are close. In our recipes, we focus on good, whole foods that are naturally lower in carbohydrates and include healthy, high-quality ingredients.

Pick and choose which recipes work for you.

We both grew up in very diverse food cultures, between us and our significant others, we include roots in several food cultures: Southern food, Californian Cuisine, Ashkenazi Jewish food, Puerto Rican and Central American foods... so you know this will be a fun party!

We hope this book of re-imagined and reworked holiday favorites makes your winter holidays much merrier!

With hope for an amazing holiday season for all!

Neisha & Kim

Notes: Helpful Things to know about the Recipes in this book

Unless otherwise specified:

Eggs: All Eggs are Large sized.

Sweeteners: Our primary sweeteners are allulose and stevia glycerite - and when brown sugar is best, we use Swerve Brown Sugar. Also, most sweetener quantities are given as a range because we don't like things as sweet as we used to, but we know we all have different preferences too. In general, the range shared is subtly sweet on the low end and moderately sweet on the high end. Feel free to adjust to your preferences.

Spices: We are both "spice with your heart" kinda gals, so feel free to tweak to suit your tastes.

Serving Sizes: All are approximate as we don't know how much food is appropriate for your meal and if you are using something as more of a main or a side, we used average size, but it's not the gospel! Adjust accordingly.

Temperatures: All are Farenheit.

In many recipes, we specify to use room temperature eggs and/or other ingredients. When we say to do it, it matters to the result. You can bring eggs to room temp faster by putting them in a bowl of lukewarm water.

Speaking of temperatures, everything in this book not being served reasonably soon after cooking should be stored in the fridge as there are no preservatives added to make out of fridge storage safe.

Frequently used abbreviations:
HWC = Heavy Whipping Cream
T = American Tablespoon
tsp = Teaspoon
c = Cup

HAPPY COOKING!

Orange Cranberry Muffins

Orange and Cranberry are a classic pairing for a reason, they make the other so much more delicious!

Makes 8 Muffins

Note: if you use allulose, it makes the exterior darker (more browned) than if you use erythritol. Adjust color expectations accordingly!

Recipe

- 3/4 c Fine Almond Flour
- 2 T Coconut Flour
- 1/3 - 1/2 c Allulose
- 1 tsp Baking Powder
- 1/2 tsp Baking Soda
- 3 T Plain Egg White Protein Powder (vanilla dairy protein ok too)
- 3 Eggs
- 3 T HWC (or coconut milk for dairy free)
- 3 T Butter, very soft (or coconut oil for dairy free)
- 1 tsp Vanilla
- 3-4 drops Stevia Glycerite (or a bit more allulose)
- 3/4 tsp Orange Extract (can be omitted, but it adds important flavor!)
- 1 tsp grated lemon peel
- 1 oz Chopped Walnuts
- 3 oz Cranberries (leave some whole and chop some in half.)

Directions

- Preheat oven to 325. Line 8 cupcake cups with paper liners, or use silicone liners on a cookie sheet.

- Wash cranberries and set them aside, discarding any yucky-looking ones.

- Take out 2 medium bowls. Put the dry ingredients (the first 6 ingredients) in one bowl. Mix to combine.

- Add butter and all other ingredients except the berries and nuts in the second bowl and beat to combine.

- Mix wet and dry together. Fold in the cranberries and nuts.

- Fill cupcakes to 3/4 full.

- Bake for 21-24 minutes, until the top is lightly browned. Cool.

- Store leftovers in the fridge. Bring to room temp before serving.

Eggnog French Toast

Bring the indulgence! One of the problems with egg based Keto breads is that they are not absorbent like traditional bread, so you don't get that bread pudding custardy effect with keto french toast, we fixed that by making this bread recipe come out perfect for french toast. This version is made festive by the addition of eggnog and cranberry flavors!

Makes 4 good-sized servings.

Recipe

Bread

- 8 eggs, room temp, separated
- 1/2 tsp cream of tartar
- 1 tsp coconut flour
- 2 oz Cream Cheese, room temp
- 6 drops Stevia Glycerite
- Optional: 1 T Allulose
- 1 tsp Vanilla

Eggnog Sauce

- 1 c Heavy Whipping Cream
- 3 Egg Yolks
- 2 T Allulose
- 1 tsp vanilla
- pinch of Nutmeg (freshly grated is best)

Cranberry Topping

- 1/2 bag Cranberries
- 1/2 c water
- 2 T Allulose (It's designed to be tart, can add more sweetener if desired)

Additional Ingredients

- 1 Whole Egg
- 1/4 c Heavy Whipping Cream
- Butter for frying French Toast

- To serve: Dusting Sweetener to garnish

Directions

- Make the bread: Preheat oven to 325. Line a large bread pan with parchment paper.

- Separate eggs , put egg whites in a mixing bowl and yolks in a medium bowl.

Eggnog French Toast

- Make the bread: Preheat oven to 325. Line a large bread pan with parchment paper.

- Separate eggs - put egg whites in a mixing bowl and yolks in a medium bowl.

- Take the bowl with yolks and add everything else on the bread list except the cream of tartar. Beat until smooth. Set aside.

- Using an electric mixer or stand mixer, beat whites on medium until they turn frothy. Add cream of tartar and turn up to high. Beat to STIFF peaks. If you don't know what that is supposed to look like, google Martha Stewart Egg Whites for a tutorial.

- Fold the yolk mixture into whites, combining well but retaining as much fluff as possible. Pour into the prepared pan.

- Bake 32-37 minutes until no wetness remains in the center. Set aside to cool.

- While that's baking, make Cranberry and Eggnog Sauce

- Cranberry: Combine all ingredients in a small saucepan. Cook on medium-high for about 10 minutes. Set aside to cool.

- Eggnog Sauce: Combine all ingredients in a room-temperature saucepan. Whisking constantly, begin to heat on medium. Make sure to scrape bottom so it does not burn. As it heats it will start to thicken. Let thicken for 5-6 minutes, until it's a custard consistency. Remove from heat and cool to room temperature.

- Pour half into a flat bottom bowl and pour the other into a minor serving pitcher.

Eggnog French Toast

- FT Batter: Add 1/4 c heavy cream and 1 whole egg to the eggnog sauce in a bowl, and beat well.

- Slice the ends off the bread, and cut the remaining pieces into 12 slices.

- Heat a nonstick frying pan with 1 T butter to medium-high.

- Dredge each slice of bread in the french toast batter to coat well—place in a frying pan. Repeat until the pan is full but not over-crowded. Fry for 2-3 minutes, until nicely browned, flip and repeat.

- Continue this pattern until all the french toast is fried. Replenish butter as needed.

TO SERVE:

- Layer 3 slices of french toast, and shake some sweetener over the top to give it a snowy appearance.

- Either serve with sauces on the side to allow folks to help themselves, or top with a pour of eggnog sauce and a spoonful of cranberry.

Apple Pie Waffles

Bright, warm fall flavors with crisp waffles! What a celebratory breakfast. And it's made keto because we've subbed zucchini for apples! Sounds funny, but tastes like apple!

Makes 2 good-sized servings.

Recipe

Waffles

- 4 eggs
- 1 T coconut flour
- 1 T pork panko (ground pork rinds)
- 1 T egg white protein powder
- 1 tsp baking soda
- 4-5 drops of stevia glycerite
- 2 T melted butter
- optional: 1 tsp Allulose

Additional Ingredients

- To serve: 1/4 c Sour Cream, Greek Yogurt, or Coconut Yogurt

"Apple" Topping

- 1 Large Zucchini
- 2 T Butter
- 1-2 T Brown Sugar Swerve
- 2 T water
- Juice of 1/2 a lemon
- pinch ground cinnamon
- pinch ground ginger
- 2-3 drops Stevia Glycerite (can omit, I find mixing sweeteners improves results)
- 1/4 tsp Apple Extract (I forgot to add this once, was still delicious and my brain told me it was apple-tasting because all the other elements were there!)

Apple Pie Waffles

Directions

- Start by making the topping: Peel and cut zucchini into quarters (the long way) and cut out the seedy center completely. Now slice the long spears into even thinner pieces, 1-2 more times depending on how big your zucchinis were. (So you have zucchini fries) Now chop into little bite-sized pieces by cutting across long pieces. The smaller the pieces the softer the filling will be and the faster it will cook.

- Put Butter in a large nonstick pan on medium heat, add zucchini, and cook 4-5 minutes, add lemon, spices, water, and sweetener and cook another 5-10 mins, until comes to your desired "doneness" add more water if it starts to dry out. It should be saucy but not soupy when finished. Taste, and add more spices and sweetener if needed. Cook another minute to incorporate additions. Cover and let sit.

- Make the waffles: Beat all ingredients together. Let sit for 1 minute then beat again until most lumps are gone.

- Prep a waffle iron, I use a mini Dash, which is nonstick.

- When the iron is ready pour the appropriate amount in the iron, close, and cook for 2-4 minutes (shorter for a soft waffle, longer for a crisp surface). Repeat until all batter is used up.

- To serve: Spoon topping over waffles, top with a heaping tablespoon of topping of choice.

Festive Crustless Quiche

Crustless Quiche (aka Frittata) is a fabulous PHD food. A base of eggs and cheese plus whatever flavor additions you want. We made this one green and red for obvious reasons, but feel free to make it your own!

I used broccoli rabe, which is incredibly low in carbs. If you can't find it, broccolini or chopped broccoli will work in its place (though higher in carbs). If you've never had broccoli rabe it's worth trying. It's far more bitter than broccoli, but pairs super well with pork sausage!

Recipe

- 16 oz broccoli rabe
- 12 oz ground Italian pork sausage OR ground pork with generous pinch of onion salt
- 1 clove garlic, minced
- 1 T olive oil
- 2 oz romano pecorino cheese or parmesan cheese, grated (skip if DF)
- Red pepper flakes to taste
- 6 eggs
- ¼ cup heavy whipping cream (can use 2 T coconut milk + 2 T almond milk for dairy-free)
- 1/2 c diced red pepper

Festive Crustless Quiche

Directions

- Preheat oven to 350°F

- Pan type: if you want thicker slices to eat as a meal with a fork, use an 8x8 pan. Using it as finger food for a party, use a 9 x 11 pan.

- Cut bottoms off Broccoli Rabe and rinse very well. Cut into roughly thirds (if using regular broccoli, cut into bite-sized pieces). Boil salted water in a pot and add Broccoli Rabe, boil for 3-4 minutes, and drain. Squeeze out water.

- Add olive oil to a pan, cook garlic for 30 seconds, add sausage, and cook.

- If using red pepper flakes, add.

- Then add the prepped Broccoli Rabe, stir, and heat through.

- Remove from heat and put into a casserole dish (size described above). Top with cheese.

- In another bowl, beat eggs and cream and pinch salt and pepper. Pour over the top so that the cheese is just submerged. Sprinkle top with red bell pepper. Bake 25-35 minutes until the top is brown and the casserole is set. Serve warm or at room temperature.

Broccoli Rabe

Leftovers Monte Cristo

I can remember my first Monte Cristo - a sandwich on french toast? Genius! We added cranberry to this one, and the bright note elevates the sandwich to extra yum!

The recipe is for 1 sandwich.

Recipe

- Sandwich Filling (for each sandwich):
- Dijon Mustard
- I slice Cheese (swiss or white cheddar)
- 3 oz Leftover Turkey
- 1 -2 oz thin cut ham
- 2 T leftover Cranberry sauce or Nature's Hollow or Good Good Jam
- 2 Slices of French Toast (recipe follows)

Directions

- Lay a slice of french toast on plate, spread with dijon, top with meat and cheese. Pop in microwave 20 seconds to melt cheese. You can also put it in a nonstick pan with lid to heat, then top with cranberry and second piece of french toast.

Classic French Toast

Similar to the Eggnog French Toast, minus the Eggnog flavors

Bread
- 8 eggs, room temp, separated
- 1/2 tsp cream of tartar
- 1 tsp coconut flour
- 2 oz Cream Cheese, softenened
- 6 drops Stevia Glycerite
- Optional: 1 T Allulose

Other
- 3 whole Egg
- 1/4 c HWC
- 1/4 c other milk (such as almond)

- Butter for frying French Toast

Directions

- Preheat oven to 325. Line a large bread pan with parchment paper.

- Separate eggs - put whites in a mixing bowl and Yolks in a medium bowl.

- Take the bowl with yolks and add everything else on the bread list except the cream of tartar. Beat until smooth. Set aside.

- Using an electric mixer or stand mixer, beat whites on medium until they turn frothy. Add cream of tartar and turn up to high. Beat to STIFF peaks. (It's crucial not to under-beat eggs, the structure of bread relies on this)

- Fold the yolk mixture into whites, combining well but retaining as much fluff as possible. Pour into the prepared pan.

- FT Batter: In a flat bottom bowl, beat together eggs, cream, and milk

- Slice the ends off the bread, and cut the remaining pieces into 12 slices. (At this stage you can wrap and freeze and have slices ready on demand!)

- Heat a nonstick frying pan with 1 T butter to medium-high.

- Dredge each slice of bread in the french toast batter to coat well—place in a frying pan. Repeat until the pan is full but not over-crowded. Fry for 2-3 minutes, until nicely browned, flip and repeat. Repeat with the rest of the bread, and replenish the butter as needed.

Sausage Balls

Lil balls of savory sausage cheesy goodness. These are definitely a party pleaser, but you don't need to plan a party as an excuse to make these. They make a great anytime meal!

Makes 24 small bites.

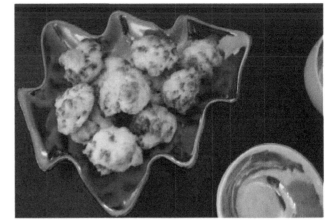

Recipe

- 4 oz Cream Cheese, room temperature
- 2 eggs, room temperature
- 4 T Pork Panko (ground pork rinds)
- 4 tsp Coconut Flour
- 2 T grated Parmesan or almond flour
- 3-4 drops of Stevia Glycerite
- 1 tsp baking Powder
- 8 oz Cooked Sausage, broken down into small pieces
- 3 oz White Cheddar, shredded
- Optional: 2 oz Cranberries, chopped

Directions

- Preheat oven to 350 and prep a baking sheet with parchment.

- Beat cream cheese and eggs until smooth, add pork panko, coconut flour, parm, stevia, and baking powder, and beat smooth. Fold in meat and shredded cheese, and cranberries if using.

- Using a teaspoon, drop into small mounds onto parchment. Wet hand slightly to smooth shape, if needed.

- Bake 350 for 16-20 minutes. Let cool.

Deviled Eggs

Deviled eggs are always welcome at the buffet! The inclusion of bacon elevating this to a work of art!

Makes 12 individual halves

Recipe

- 6 Large Eggs - hardboiled
- 1 T Dijon Mustard
- 3 slices Cooked Bacon
- 1 -2 Scallions or bunch of chives
- Salt and Pepper
- Paprika for dusting
- 1/2 c Neisha's Bacon Mayo (or other good quality mayo)

Directions

- Take eggs and carefully slice them in half lengthwise. Remove the yolk and put it in a bowl. Add Mayo, Mustard, salt, and pepper to yolks and mash and mix.

- Spoon or pipe (using a pastry bag or a plastic bag with the corner cut off) into each cavity in the white.

- Arrange on your serving plate.

- Dice the onion and bacon. Sprinkle over top of eggs, making sure most sticks to the yolk filling.

- Sprinkle with Paprika for color.

- Chill in the fridge for at least 2 hours before serving. It can be made a day ahead.

Bacon Mayo

Recipe

- 1/2 c Bacon Grease (in liquid form, so needs to be warm but not hot)
- 1 Egg Yolk
- 1 Tbsp lemon juice
- 1 tsp Mustard
- Generous pinch of salt and pepper

Directions

- Cook half a pound of bacon, remove bacon strips, and set aside.

- Pour bacon fat into a tall narrow jar that fits your immersion blender head.

- Add all other ingredients. Place blender head on the bottom (with yolk underneath head) and turn on high to emulsify and mayo-nize! It just takes a few seconds.

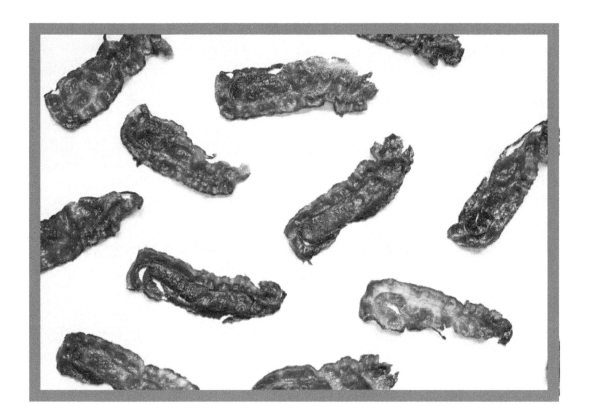

Lemony Lox Bites

Lemon and Dill are a heavenly combination - this recipe makes great use of both!
These are great make-ahead brunch treats or party hors d'oeuvres! A great alternative to bagels with Lox!

Recipe

- 1-2 large Cucumbers, preferably English
- 8 oz Cream Cheese, softened
- Juice of 1 Lemon (zest it first and set aside for topping)
- 1 T minced Fresh Dill
- 1 tsp minced Fresh Chives
- Pinch Salt
- 5 oz Smoked Salmon/Lox

Garnish/Toppings
- More Fresh Dill
- Lemon Zest (zest the lemon before you juice it or it's a mess)
- Pepper
- If you love capers, feel free to add some minced to the toppings!

Lemony Lox Bites

Directions

- Make the flavored cream cheese:
  - Take the slightly softened cream cheese, put it in a bowl, and add lemon juice, salt, and minced dill. Beat to fluff up. Set aside. (this stuff is delicious)

- Slice cucumber very thin (I use a mandolin). Sprinkle with salt.

- Apply a small spoonful of cream cheese to the cucumber.

- Cut salmon into rectangles to fit your cucumber rounds, and place on cream cheese. This doesn't have to be exact.

- Arrange on your serving dish and sprinkle with dill and lemon zest.

- You can make it many hours ahead, keep it in the fridge covered until ready to serve.

Shrimp and Sauces

Bright and tangy cocktail sauce! Rich and creamy tartar sauce! All without the added sugar we usually get? WIN! Big beautiful shrimp dipped in yummy sauces makes for a great appetizer or even full meal.
Make the sauce ahead, and you've got this ready in no time at all!

Makes 8 appetizers or 4 meals.

Recipe

- 1 Pound of frozen pre-cooked Jumbo Shrimp (peeled & deveined, tail on)
- Keto Cocktail Sauce (recipe follows)
- Keto Tartar Sauce (recipe follows)
- Lemon Wedges for serving garnish
- Optional: sprinkle flat-leaf parsley for color

Directions

- Put frozen shrimp in a colander, and let sit in the sink with cool water running over it until the shrimp is no longer frozen, just chilled.

- Pat dry. Sprinkle with some salt and some parsley if you want a bit of color.

- Arrange prettily on a plate and serve with a side of Keto tartar sauce and Keto cocktail sauce.

Sauces: Tartar and Cocktail

COCKTAIL SAUCE

- 1/2 c Primal Kitchen Unsweetened Ketchup or other Keto Ketchup
- Juice of 1 lemon
- 1/4 to 1/2 tsp jarred horseradish
- ¼ tsp Primal Kitchen Steak Sauce or Worcestershire sauce
- Stevia Glycerite to taste (or another sweetener) OMIT if using sweetened ketchup or it will be over-sweet!

- Easy peasy. Put Ketchup and lemon juice in a small bowl, add the smallest amount of horseradish, taste, and up to the level of intensity. Then sweeten to balance the flavor. Add just a drop at a time. Don't oversweeten, if you do, add a bit more ketchup. If you use an already sweetened Keto Ketchup, omit the sweetener. You want this a little sweet, not full sweet!

- Store in fridge til ready to use.

TARTAR SAUCE

- 1/2 c Good Mayo (recipe follows) OR Chosen Foods Mayonnaise
- 1 T minced Dill Pickle
- 1 T minced chives or 1 tsp minced scallion
- ½ T chopped Fresh Dill
- ½ tsp Dijon Mustard
- Juice of half a lemon

- Mix all ingredients. Onion/chive flavors will intensify overnight.

- Store in fridge til ready to use.

Good Mayo Recipe

Recipe

- 1 cup Avocado Oil –

I recommend Chosen Foods brand for best flavor

- 2 egg yolks
- generous pinch salt
- 3 T fresh lemon juice
- 1-2 tsp Dijon mustard

Equipment:
Immersion blender and a jar JUST big enough to fit the head in –

Directions

- I am not kidding about the jar just fitting the blender head. Any major gap and it doesn't work. But when it fits right it works like magic.

- Put yolks in a jar. Add all other ingredients except oil. Then pour in the oil on top.

- Immerse the head of the immersion blender so it touches the bottom of the jar. Turn on HIGH and watch it become mayo!

- It starts right away. Move your head up and down a bit to make it all mayo'ed.

- It should turn from a bunch of ingredients to a white (or off-white depending on mustard) thick opaque emulsion. Taste the mayo- it probably needs a bit more salt.

- Will keep in the fridge for 1 week.

This mayo is great with additions like chopped garlic or basil or dill... spice it up.
And... if you just can't be bothered, Chosen Foods Mayo isn't bad. Not as good, but not bad.

Party Mix

Message from Niesha!
BE WARNED!! THIS IS DANGEROUSLY GOOD! IT'S VERY EASY TO OVEREAT AND SHOULD ONLY BE MADE AS A TREAT ON RARE OCCASIONS. ESPECIALLY IF YOU ARE LIKE ME AND ARE SENSITIVE TO NUTS!

This recipe does not give quantities of spices; you are meant to customize it to your tastes. This dish should be highly spiced and salty.

Recipe

- 6 pieces Sliced Smoked Gouda
- 8 (or more) Strips of Bacon, reserve grease
- 16 oz of salted mixed nuts
- 8 oz of salted cashews (you can do whole or halves)
- 12 oz of pistachios (already shelled)
- 2 boxes Fat Snax Sea Salt crackers (or make more sliced cheese crackers)
- 1 stick Butter, melted (if not using fat snax, just homemade cheese crisps, use 1/2 stick butter)
- 2 T of Worcestershire sauce
- 1-2 tsp Hot Sauce (optional)
- A lot of Garlic powder, Smoked paprika, onion powder, chili powder, Redmonds salt, or Redmonds seasoning salt.

Party Mix

Directions

- PREHEAT OVEN TO 350 for Gouda Crackers

- Cut gouda slices into cracker-sized squares. Place pieces on a cookie sheet on top of parchment paper. Bake for 8- 10 min or until the cheese is bubbled up. A little brown is perfect just don't let them burn. I recommend watching them closely as different cheeses will cook differently. You want them WELL BAKED. This is what makes them good and crispy. Allow them to cool while making the rest of the mix. After they are cooled they will be wonderfully CRISPY! Set aside.

- Cook bacon extra crispy. Chop into large bite-sized pieces. Feel free to make more, because, more bacon is never wrong. Reserve fat to pour over the party mix.

- In a large casserole-type pan or big sheet pan (or two) distribute just the nuts and fat snax crackers (do not include homemade cheese crackers).

- In a separate bowl combine: melted butter, Worcestershire sauce, hot sauce (if using), and bacon fat.

- Spoon some butter sauce over mix, then top with a generous shake of the spices—then pour over reserved bacon fat. Toss and give another pass with spices.

- Bake at 250 for 1 hour. Stir nuts & crackers every 15 mins or so and add more seasonings.

- Remove from oven but while still hot, mix in cheese crisps and bacon pieces. Add more seasoning if desired. Toss.

- Let cool for about 30 minutes and serve!

Charcuterie Board

HOW DO YOU CHARCUTERIE?

it starts with the board: You'll want a large wood cutting board... though you can also use a platter or large plate in a pinch!

TJ Maxx Home Goods and antique/second-hand shops are my favorite places to shop for boards. To make the board look more interesting, and contain little items like olives, or add sauces/mustards, you'll need some small bowls as well. Antique shops are great places to get unique little spoons, plates, and serving pieces.

Please keep it simple, don't overcomplicate it.

Get creative with your board, there is literally NO WAY for you to mess this up. Unless you eat everything before your guests arrive. I'm guilty of going in on the olives a bit early myself.

Pick what you like:

- Cured meats - we like prosciutto, summer sausage, and peppered salami.
- Cheeses – we love brie, smoked gouda, red dragon, and blueberry goat cheese.
- Nuts - we like pistachios & cashews.
- Olives: Our favorite olives are garlic-stuffed & blue cheese stuffed.
- Keto Crackers - you can buy these or make your own (recipes in the book)
- Keto Jelly or Jam - Nature's Hollow or Good Good are two brands
- Sauces (fancy mustard is my favorite pick)
- Berries - raspberries, blueberries, & strawberries
- Pickles or Cornichons
- Bell Peppers (different colors for a variation on the board)
- Liver Pate or Liver Mousse (recipe in the book!)
- Jerky or Carnivore Crisps
- Fried Chicken Skins
- Fresh Herbs as garnish and add a lovely aroma to the board

Charcuterie Board

Directions

Arranging the board :
- I put the bowls on the board first to get a rough layout.
- Then I place the cheese.

- Then I arrange my meats, folding the ones that are larger to look nice and take up less space depending on the size of your board.

- Once you have done that you can fill in the spaces with herbs, crackers, berries, etc. Make sure to have cheese knives and toothpicks for serving purposes. Enjoy!

Julie's Famous Chicken Liver Mousse

One of Ken Berry's Superfoods: LIVER! He is always excited when Liver is on the menu in a way that tastes amazing! Iffy on the idea of liver, this is an easy transition. It's chicken liver, which is milder than beef. Double the recipe if feeding a crowd, it also freezes well.

It should make 8 good sized servings.

This recipe was adapted from the talented Julie Fox-McClure who makes the fantastic Fox Hill Kitchens, Bagels Buns and Crisps! (A totally PHD approved product line!) In fact, her mini bagel holes are amazing heavily toasted and spread with the mousse and her crisps are a wonderful assortment of crackers.

Recipe

- 1/2 lb Raw Chicken Livers
- 1/2 lb Butter (we use Kerrygold salted in this) softened
- About 1.5 oz Minced Shallots* (which is 2-3 average-sized ones)
- 4 T Cognac or Dry Sherry (Cognac has fewer carbs)
- Fresh Thyme, 2-3 stems worth- use the leaves, discard stems.
- Pinch dried Majoram
- Salt & Pepper
- Small pinch of Allspice or Cloves (allspice is a bit milder)

- To add while blending:
- Juice and zest of 1/2 lemon
- 2-4 T Heavy Whipping Cream

Yes, shallots are higher carbs than other onions, but they add incredible flavor to this dish. You're not eating many per serving, but you could use yellow onion instead.

Julie's Famous
Chicken Liver Mousse

Directions

- Add 4 T of the butter to a pan and cook livers, laying them flat side on the pan, cook 2 minutes, flip, and cook another 2. Stir, cooking one more minute or so until they are no longer red, but still pink in the center. Feel free to cut one to check. Do not overcook.

- Remove livers and set aside, add another 4 T butter to the pan and add shallots and begin to cook, after 2-3 minutes, add herbs and spices, and alcohol. Cook until shallots are translucent and some alcohol has cooked off.

- Pour everything cooked so far into a good blender, scraping the pan to get it all. Cover blender but remove the center, and cover the hole with a clean kitchen towel and blend, slowly adding remaining butter through the hole in the lid as it's blending.

- Once you've added the butter, add lemon and cream. Stop the blender once incorporated and the mix has gone silky. The texture should be very smooth. If too thick, add more lemon and/or cream, as desired.

- Taste. Add more salt or other spices if needed. You want the seasoning fairly strong as it mellows as it chills. Don't be alarmed if the liver tastes more livery than you like. That also mellows as it chills. You can't add more ingredients once chilled, so now is your chance to tinker!

- When the taste is right, pour through a fine strainer to refine the texture, then transfer into your desired serving container.

- Let chill, covered, in the fridge for a few hours, overnight is great!

- If you are not eating within a day or so, melt some butter and pour a layer of butter on top to keep sealed and fresh.

Bacon Jam & Baked Brie

Yep. Bacon Jam. With Brie. Savory goodness. Salty sumptuous umami flavors come together with gooey chewy textures for a perfect bite of happy.

Recipe

- Round of Brie
- 1 lb bacon
- 14 oz Can Diced tomatoes, drain out the liquid
- Large Yellow Onion, diced
- 1/2 tsp Smoked Paprika
- 1 T Apple Cider Vinegar
- optional: pinch Cayenne, Swerve brown sugar sweetener

JAM

- Thinly chop bacon (I just leave it stacked like it came out of the package. No need to separate and chop slices individually!)
- Heat a skillet and fry the bacon crispy, using a slotted spoon, remove the bacon but leave the fat in the pan.
- Add onion to the pan, and cook until translucent and browned. Remove using a slotted spoon. Pour off extra bacon fat (no need to clean the pan, you just want liquid removed)
- Return drained bacon and onion to pan. Add drained tomatoes and spices. Cook until the tomatoes are soft and the consistency of a thick sauce is achieved. Set aside until ready to serve. It should be served warm, so if you've made it ahead, warm back up before serving.

BRIE

- Take brie out of the packaging - yes the rind stays, it's edible!
- Bake in a 400-degree oven for 20 minutes for warm yet not too oozy internal brie or 30 minutes if you want the cheese runnier!
- Plate Brie then top with jam before serving. Serve with desired crackers for spreading!

Cheeseball

Big thanks to **Melissa of Cooking Keto with Faith** for this party pleaser!

Recipe

- 2 x 8 oz packs of cream cheese
  (you may use goat cheese if you prefer)
- 8 strips cooked bacon (chopped)
- 1 cup shredded mild cheddar
- 1/4 cup green olives with pimentos (sliced into small pieces)
- 2 TBSP chives (chopped)
- 1 to 2 TBSP FLAVOR GODS RANCH SEASONING (use how much you like, start at 1 TBSP) or use the homemade ranch recipe on the bottom of the page.

Directions

- Put all ingredients into a med/large mixing bowl.

- Use a hand mixer to incorporate all the ingredients together.

- Shape into a ball and plastic wrap the cheese ball. Place into the refrigerator for at least 1 Hr. for all the flavors to marry.

- Unwrap the cheese ball and allow it to come to room temperature for at least 30 minutes before serving, so the cheese ball becomes spreadable.

- serve with "cracker" of choice (see cracker section!)

Ranch Seasoning

Mix together and store in glass container away from light to maintain flavor

- 2 tsp Dried parsley
- 1 tsp Dried dill
- 1 tsp Dried chives
- 1/2 tsp Garlic powder
- 1/2 tsp Onion powder
- 1/2 tsp Sea salt
- 1/4 tsp Black pepper

Crackers

When making dips and spreads, sometimes you want a crispy delivery device like a cracker!

On the following, pages are recipes for some of our favorite versions, but there are also some acceptable store-bought options! Because sometimes you don't have time to muck about!

We like...

Pork Rinds/Chiccharones

Carnivore Crips Chicken Breast- not much flavor, but that makes them perfect for topping with a flavorful cheese or spread!

Carnivore Snax Chicken Chips - like a triscuit made of Chicken!

Fat Snax Crackers

Flackers - flax seed crackers

Fathead Crackers

For fun, I cut these out with star cookie cutters, but you can cut them into squares with a knife or pizza cutter if you don't want to get as fancy. If cutting stars or any other shape with points, be aware the edges can burn if you don't watch them!

Recipe

- 8 oz Mozzarella Cheese, shredded
- 1 oz Cream Cheese
- 1 cup Almond Flour, plus an extra sprinkle
- 1 egg
- pinch salt
- optional flavor additions (choose what works with your planned spreads!): chopped fresh rosemary, onion powder, everything seasoning...

Directions

- Put cheeses in a microwave-safe bowl and microwave in 30-second increments until melted, mix with a fork.

- Add egg and beat together with cheese, add 1 cup almond flour (and any seasonings of choice) and knead into the cheese mix. You'll want to use your (clean) hands. When comes together as a ball of dough it's ready. Scatter some extra almond flour on the cutting board and sprinkle some on top of the dough and roll out to the desired thickness of the crackers.

- If the dough gets too cold, it will be hard to roll, simply pop it back in a bowl in the microwave for 15 or so seconds to warm up so it's pliable again.

- Once you have the dough rolled out, cut out shapes as desired. I used cookie cutters, but you can just cut them in rectangles. Move to a parchment-lined baking sheet and bake at 350 for 8 minutes. Flip and bake another 2-3 minutes to slightly brown both sides.

- Serve! (They store fine in the fridge. I like to toast them back up before serving. just pop it in a warm oven for a few minutes to do so!)

Gouda Crisps

We Americans say this type of cheese - "Goo-da" but if you were a native Dutch speaker, you'd say it "How-da!"

This cheese is named after a town in Holland and is one of the favorite cheeses of the Netherlands, and we think for a good reason!

Recipe

- A bunch of Gouda Slices

Directions

- Preheat oven to 350, and top a baking sheet with parchment.

- Cut gouda slices into cracker-sized squares.

- Place pieces on a cookie sheet on top of parchment paper, and make sure there's no overlap. Bake for 8- 10 min or until the cheese is bubbled up. A little brown is perfect just don't let them burn. I recommend watching them closely as different cheeses will cook differently. You want them WELL BAKED. This is what makes them good and crispy.

- After they are cooled they will be wonderfully CRISPY! Set aside.

Hemp Crisps

Crispy, wheaty (without actual wheat) nuttiness in a cracker! I accidentally invented these crackers when trying to make a tortilla, but instead made a giant crisp cracker!

You can flavor this recipe however you want, I used everything seasoning, but you could make them plain without the seasoning, or add just onion powder, or whatever suits you!

Recipe

- 1.25 c Water
- 1 c Hemp Hearts
- 1 tsp Coconut Flour
- 4 T Gelatin
- 1 tsp everything seasoning or other
- Pinch Salt

Directions

- Put water in a saucepan, and sprinkle the gelatin over the top in as even a layer as you can. Let sit cold, for about 5 minutes to allow the gelatin to bloom. Turn on the heat, and whisk until liquid and smooth, like a frothy egg white. Turn off the heat. Mix in hemp hearts, coconut flour, and seasonings

- Let cool a minute or two, it will "thicken" - if you accidentally let it sit and it's now too thick, reheat a bit. You want it to be thick enough that it won't run all over the baking sheet when spooning it out.

- Spoon into small flat rounds on a parchment-lined cookie sheet, sprinkle a pinch of salt on top, and bake until brown and crispy - about 20 mins at 350.

- They need to look well-browned, but not burnt. If they are still pale, they'll be chewy, not crispy. Carefully peel off the parchment. (the gelatin makes them stick, but they peel very quickly.)

Rainforest Crisps

There are these fabulous fancy crackers I always see on cheese trays, they are called Rain Coast crisps, but I always misremember the name as Rainforest crisps.. so when I made these copycats, I thought, "why not call them that?" So here we are.

You can make them in a variety of flavors by swapping the spices and nut types. Here are two I like.

They are a bit time and effort-consuming, just a heads up!

They do store well in the freezer. So make it in advance!

Cranberry Rosemary Pecan

Recipe

- 3.5 oz Pecans
- 1 oz Pumpkin Seeds
- 3 oz Almond Flour
- 1.5 oz Hazelnuts
- 4 oz Fresh Cranberries, dried (see directions following cracker recipe)
- 2 Tablespoons finely chopped Fresh Rosemary leaves
- 2 T Flaxseed
- 1 Egg, beaten
- 1/4 to 1/2 cup water
- 1 tsp Baking Soda
- Pinch Salt
- 2-3 Tablespoons Brown Sugar Swerve
- 1/4 c water

Rainforest Crisps

Directions

- Put Flax seeds and 1 oz of pecans into a coffee grinder and process just enough to turn to flour (if you over grind the oil in the nuts comes out and makes a sort of a paste) so err on the side of under rather than over.

- Place water, egg, and salt and swerve into a bowl and beat together.

- Finely chop all remaining nuts and the dried cranberries. (If nuts are too big when you slice crackers will tend to crumble rather than slice cleanly) Add to bowl, chopped rosemary, powdered pecans, flax, and almond flour. Mix well. Should form a nutty dough. If it seems too dry, add 1 Tablespoon of water at a time until the mixture comes together.

- Grease or non-stick spray mini loaf pans and pack the dough into each, press in so it's tight and level with the loaf pan top.

- Bake 325 for 30ish minutes, until golden on top. Let cool completely before removing from loaf pans. Once cool, set it in the freezer for an hour or so before the next step.

- With a very sharp knife, carefully slice into thin crackers. They'll want to crumble rather than slice cleanly, so be patient.

- Turn oven to 275. Lay slices onto a rack-topped cookie sheet and bake another 20 minutes or so, until they start to get more intensely brown (keep an eye on them you don't want them burning) If you do not have a rack, you can bake for 10 minutes then carefully flip and bake another 10 minutes the other side.

- Let cool **completely** before moving. (Important!) Store well in the freezer, so feel free to make it in advance!

Rainforest Crisps

Brown Nutty Crackers

Recipe

Reminiscent of pumpernickel or that sweet brown bread they serve at Cheesecake Factory.

- 2 oz Pecans
- 1 oz Sunflower seeds
- 2 oz Almond Flour
- 2 Tablespoons Black Cocoa (can use regular unsweetened, but the color will be lighter)
- 2 oz Hazelnuts
- 2 T Flaxseed
- 1 Egg, beaten
- 1/4 to 1/2 cup water
- 1 tsp Baking Soda
- Pinch Salt
- 2-3 Tablespoons Brown Sugar Swerve

Directions

- Follow the same instructions as in the previous recipe, but grind all the pecans to use as "flour", rather than just some of them.

- Knowing when toasted will be a bit more challenging as they begin with a dark color, so take care not to let them burn!

Dried Cranberries

It's almost impossible to find dried cranberries without sugar added. I make my own and they are great! Here's how:

- Wash and dry a bag of cranberries, and discard any yucky ones.
- Cut all cranberries in half. Put in a bowl.
- Toss with 1 tsp avocado oil and 2 T allulose (more if you want sweeter).
- Lay out on a parchment-covered baking sheet
- Put in a 200-degree oven for 90 minutes. Check them. You want them to have shrunk and become dryer, not dried out. If you over-dry them, they lose their flavor. Most recipes overcook them in my opinion!
- Store in the freezer until ready to use.

2

3

4

5

Pumpkin Peppers

Beckett loves to cook! It's always fun to have fun recipes you can do with the kiddos!

Picadillo is a delicious easy ground beef recipe, that uses Puerto Rican sofrito as its base seasoning. One of my favorite ways to make ground beef. But today we are going to add some holiday flare and make Jack-o-lantern stuffed pepper with this delicious beef recipe based on my Abuelita's recipe.

Makes 6 Peppers.

Recipe

- 6 Orange Bell Peppers
- 1 lb. ground beef
- 2 tbsp olive oil (or fat of choice)
- 1/2 cup yellow onion chopped
- 1/3 cup green bell pepper seeded & chopped
- 1/3 cup red bell pepper seeded & chopped
- 1/3 cup sofrito (homemade is best you can use store-bought but it's NOT as good and will not flavor the beef as well)
- 1/3 cup canned tomato sauce
- 1/4 cup olives with pimento sliced or whole (personal preference)
- cilantro for garnish
- salt to taste

SOFRITO INGREDIENTS: makes a storable amount (more than used here)
- 2 large green bell peppers roughly chopped and seeded
- 1 large onion roughly chopped
- 1/2 red bell pepper seeded and roughly chopped
- 1 head of garlic, peeled and roughly chopped
- 2 bunches of cilantro roughly chopped
- 1 pinch of salt

39

Kid Friendly

Pumpkin Peppers

Directions

- Make the Sofrito: Put all the ingredients into a blender or food processor and pulse into a coarse paste.
- Store in an airtight container in the refrigerator if using within a few weeks or freeze for more extended storage.

- GROUND BEEF INSTRUCTIONS
- Start by adding the olive oil or fat of choice inside a medium-sized pan over medium to high heat. Sauté the sofrito for two to three minutes. After your sofrito is slightly brown, turn down the heat to low-medium, and add in the yellow onion with the bell pepper chopped mix. Stir occasionally for two to three minutes.

- Pour in your tomato sauce, and sliced olives, and add your ground beef. Stir the picadillo until it is evenly mixed and bring heat to medium. Cover the pan to hold in moisture and cook the beef faster.

- Uncover the pan occasionally to stir the picadillo. Once the beef is browned and well done, you may lower the heat to reach your desired sauce consistency. However, the picadillo should not be runny. Salt to taste.

- PEPPERS: Cut each pepper around the stem and remove it to create a lid. Remove the seeds and, if the peppers do not sit flat, trim the bottoms slightly; just be careful not to cut a hole in the bottom of the peppers. Using the tip of a small serrated knife, cut a face like a jack-o'-lantern into the side of each pepper.

- Fill the peppers with the beef mixture and put on a baking sheet with the lids on the side. Bake until the peppers are fork-tender, about 30 minutes.

Christmas Tree Pizzas

A fun and yummy project to do with your kiddos - or the young at heart. These are mini fathead pizza bites, decorated to look like little Christmas trees. A much healthier alternative to decorating Christmas cookies!

Makes 24 single bites.

Recipe

- Fat Head Dough:
  - 8 oz Mozzarella Cheese, shredded
  - 2 oz Cream Cheese
  - 1 egg
  - 1 cup Almond Flour
  - Optional seasonings: Italian Seasoning, garlic powder, etc.

- Toppings Options:
  - No added sugar Tomato Sauce/Pizza Sauce for red sauce OR Herbed Cream Cheese or spread for White Sauce
  - Red and Green Bell Peppers
  - Pepperoni
  - Mozzarella Cheese, shredded
  - Parmesan for snow
  - Spinach or Basil, cut into strips

Directions

- Make the dough - add cheeses to a microwave-safe bowl, heat in 30-second increments until melted, and stir to combine. Add egg and almond flour and knead to combine. I recommend adding some spices, as the dough is pretty plain, but up to you!

Kid Friendly

Christmas Tree Pizzas

- Once the ball of dough comes together, dust the surface with more almond flour and roll out the dough thinly. Cut out several trees using Christmas tree cookie cutters (or whatever you'd like). Place on a cookie sheet lined with parchment. If dough leftovers lose flexibility and you need to re-roll, take the leftover dough and put it back in the microwave for 10-20 seconds. Roll out again and make more shapes! Continue until the dough is used up.

- Now, pre-bake your cutouts - give them 8-10 minutes at 350 until just barely browned.

- While those are baking cut up your toppings, I like to make tiny cubes from red and green peppers that look like ornaments. You can also make light strings of pepperoni or whatever shapes suit you.

- When crusts are done, it's time to top! Flip them over on parchment and top as you like! How your family members decorate them can be a fun personality comparison!

- For these, I used pizza sauce on some, and, I spread soft cheese for a white sauce on others.

- Return to oven to melt cheese, about 5 minutes. Exposed pointy edges risk burning so keep an eye on them!

Main Dishes & Sides

Squash Soup
with browned butter and fried sage

Beautiful sunset color with a rich flavor and smooth texture. This is a crowd pleser for sure!

First, we must discuss squashes. You can make this soup with either Sugar Pie Pumpkin or green-skinned Kabocha squash. You could also use butternut squash, which is a bit higher carb. then the other options, but it will work just as well in terms of flavor and texture! Orange/red Kabocha will be a bit too sweet. The intensity of the color of the soup will vary depending on the squash chosen. Kabocha will produce the most orange effect. The pumpkin will be a more mellow yellow.

If serving as an appetizer for a holiday meal, I suggest small bowls so folks don't get too full!

Makes 8 small servings

Recipe

- 1 large or two smaller winter squashes, such as Sugar Pie Pumpkin or Kabocha squash to make about 20 oz of peeled cubes
- 1 large onion (about 9-10 oz)
- 4 Tablespoons Salted Butter for soup, plus 2-4 T for frying Sage
- 2 Cloves Garlic
- 4 Cups Chicken Broth
- 1/4th tsp salt (more if your broth isn't salty!)
- 2 Tablespoons Cream
- 1 tsp Smoked Paprika
- 1/8 tsp Italian Seasoning
- 3/4 cup Sour Cream or Greek Yogurt thinned with 2-3 T Cream for topping
- 16 sage leaves for frying

44

Squash Soup

Directions

- First, you're going to prep the squash. If you have sensitive skin, I recommend wearing disposable gloves for this step as squash produces a sap that can stick to your skin and some folks find it irritating. It's not dangerous, and won't cause a problem with eating!

- Cut open your squash and scrape out the seeds and gunk. With a peeler, peel off the skin (if your peeler isn't up to the task, use a small knife carefully) and cut the flesh into cubes.

- Heat 4 Tablespoons of butter in a soup pot. Chop onion and saute in butter on medium until browned. Chop garlic and add to onion, cooking another 2-3 minutes. Add 3 cups of the broth to a simmer, and add the cubed squash, salt, paprika, and Italian seasoning. Cook until squash is soft. (while simmering, make fried sage - see below) Remove from heat.

- If you have an immersion blender, blend with that until smooth. If the soup seems too thick, add a bit more stock.

- If you do not have an immersion blender, let the soup cool for a few minutes - then pour it into a blender and blend, then return to the soup pot.

- Add cream and 1 Tablespoon of the browned butter from making the sage (get the browned bits!) and simmer for 2-3 more minutes. Taste the soup and add more spices as desired. The quantities of spices listed in the recipe are minimums, you can always add more to your tastes.

Squash Soup

Fried Sage:

- In a small saute pan (I use my egg pan!) melt and brown 2 Tablespoons of salted butter - don't burn the butter, but let it brown for great flavor. (if your pan is bigger you may need more butter, you need enough to cover the sage leaves)

- Pick the good-looking individual sage leaves off the bunch and drop in butter, flipping after 1-2 minutes, cooking long enough to crisp up. Move onto a plate with a paper towel. Continue until you have enough leaves to properly top your number of servings of soup. Remove butter from heat, you'll use some of the butter in the soup. Frying in butter means you need to ensure the butter doesn't burn, if it does, start with fresh butter. Browning is good and desired, just not burning.

- To serve: put soup in bowls, top with a drizzle of thinned sour cream in whatever pattern suits you.
Place 1-2 fried Sage leaves resting on the soup.

Neisha's Famous Cornbread

Sink your teeth into this salty wonder of pillowy center and crispy edges. Cornbread is the perfect side for so many winter foods! It's also the base for Neisha's cornbread dressing!

Makes 8 small servings, we recommend double or tripling for a group.

Recipe

- 4 tbsp pork panko
- 4 tsp coconut flour
- 2 tsp baking powder
- 2 tbsp almond flour
- 2 eggs (room temperature)
- 2 oz cream cheese, softened
- 2 oz butter, softened
- bacon grease or butter for the pan

Directions

- Preheat oven to 350. Grease a 6.5" cast iron skillet with fat. If using cast iron, pop it into the oven to preheat before filling for an extra crisp crust. If you do not have a cast iron skillet you can use a 7 or 8" cake pan.

- Take out two bowls:
  - In one: mix pork panko, almond flour, baking powder, and coconut flour
  - In the second bowl: Mix softened butter and cream cheese until they form a creamy texture. Add eggs and mix well.

- Combine contents of both bowls, mix well, and pour into prepped pan.
- Bake for 25 minutes at 350.

- Allow to cool before removing from pan.

Broccoli Salad

Bacon dressing?

Crumbled bacon? Cheese?

Yes, please!

Makes 8 servings

Recipe

- 8 cups broccoli cut into bite-sized pieces
- * 1 red onion diced
- * ½ cup bacon bits (or as much as you like)
- * 2 TSP of garlic powder
- * 1 cup of shredded cheddar cheese (or as much as you like)

- dressing instructions - everything should be room temperature except the bacon fat.
- * 1 cup mayo (you may also use a clean Italian dressing in place of the mayo)
- * 3 tablespoons apple cider vinegar (leave out if using Italian dressing)
- * 2 tbsp of warm bacon fat (liquid consistency)
- * salt & pepper to taste

Broccoli Salad

Directions

- In a large bowl, combine broccoli and onion and set aside.

- Cook fresh bacon to make your bacon bits. Chop bacon into small bits and add to medium heat pan. Cook until crispy or desired texture. Take bacon bits out of pan and place on a paper bowl to cool. Pour 2 tbsp of bacon fat into a bowl and add all dressing ingredients.

- Whisk together the dressing ingredients in a medium bowl.
- Pour the prepared dressing over the broccoli mixture and mix well.

- Place salad in the fridge to cool (about an hour)

- After the mixture has cooled, mix in the shredded cheese and cooled bacon bits and serve.

- Broccoli Salad can be made ahead & kept in the fridge (at least an hour but up to 24 hours) until ready to serve.

- Reserve some crisp bacon for garnish if desired and add just before serving.

Coleslaw

Coleslaw is a holiday food? It is to Kim's mom, Jane who loves coleslaw with turkey, so if there's turkey... there's coleslaw. After having grown up this way, it's not a holiday table without it!

Because Mom's version is not very Keto, Melissa has been kind enough to let us use her delicious recipe! Check out all her amazing recipes at cookingketowithfaith.com

Makes 6 servings

Recipe

- 16 oz. bag of coleslaw or 1 medium-sized cabbage shredded
- 1/2 cup keto-approved mayonnaise
- 1/4 cup sour cream (thinned with 2 TBSP of water)
- 1/4 cup heavy whipping cream
- 3 TBSP sweetener (Melissa uses a stevia and erythritol blend)
- 2 TBSP tarragon vinegar (white vinegar is also fine)
- 2 TBSP lemon juice
- 1/2 tsp salt (we use Redmonds Real Salt)
- 1/2 tsp ground black pepper
- 1/2 tsp mustard powder
- 1/4 tsp onion powder

Directions

- Pulse the coleslaw in a food processor until it is the size of rice grains, empty it into a large mixing bowl, and set aside.

- Add the rest of the ingredients into a small mixing bowl and whisk until well combined.

- Evenly pour the liquid mixture onto the coleslaw and toss through until the coleslaw is well coated

- Set aside in the refrigerator for at least 2hrs+ for the flavors to marry.

Southern Collards with Hog Jowl

A truly southern dish with all the smoky rich flavors you want in a greens dish. Bitter, buttery, salty sumptuousness! And yes, hog jowl, but if you can't find hog jowl you can use bacon instead.

Recipe

- 2 pounds of collard greens
- 3 cups water
- 3 cups bone broth of choice
- 1/2 to 1 cup chopped onion
- 8 thick slices of hog jowl, diced (you may substitute bacon)
- 1/2 teaspoon freshly ground black pepper
- 1/2 teaspoon crushed pepper flakes
- 2 teaspoons seasoned salt blend
- 1 teaspoon of garlic powder

Directions

- Wash collard greens in about 3 to 4 changes of water, until no sandy sediment can be felt at the bottom of the sink or bowl.

- Lay each leaf out and cut out the thick center stalk and any very thick veins. Layer several leaves and roll them; Cut the rolled leaves into 1/2-inch strips. You may also chop the leaves.

Southern Collards

- In a large skillet over medium heat cook the diced bacon or jowl to render some of the fat. Take out the jowl or bacon and sauté your onions. Pour off fat and save for another use.

- In a large stockpot or Dutch oven bring the 6 cups of water to a boil. Add the cooked bacon or hog jowl, the sautéed onions, salt, red and black peppers, garlic, and seasoned salt. Add the greens to boiling water. You might have to add the collard greens in batches to allow them to cook down and take up less space.

- Cover and simmer over medium-low heat for about 1 hour, or until greens are tender.

- Serve the collard greens with freshly baked keto cornbread and pass the hot pepper vinegar or pepper sauce at the table.

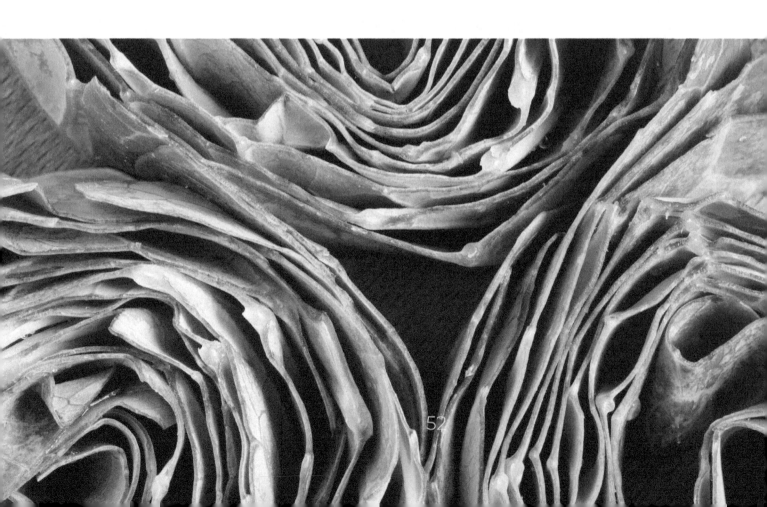

Hasselback Zucchini

Step aside Hasselback potatoes, Zucchini is where it's at! Fresh, sweet zucchini served on an herbed cheese spread.

Makes 6ish servings

Recipe

- 2 large or 4 smaller Zucchini
- 2 Tablespoons Butter, melted
- generous pinch salt
- 1/4 tsp fresh thyme (optional)
- 1/4 cup herbed soft cheese such as Boursin or Alouette
- 1 Tablespoon Parmesan

Directions

- Preheat oven to 400, and line a baking sheet with parchment.

- On a cutting board, place a zucchini between two butter knives or chopsticks so that when you slice, the cut doesn't go all the way through.

- Thinly slice zucchini leaving a bit still attached at the bottom. Move to baking sheet and repeat with remaining zucchinis.

- Pour melted butter over and season with salt and thyme. Making sure to get between slices.

- Bake for about 20-30 minutes (shorter for firmer, longer for softer)

- Spread soft cheese on a serving plate as a bed for the zucchini to sit on. Sprinkle with a pinch more salt and the parmesan. Serve!

Scalloped Fauxtatoes

Cheesy, creamy and potato-like yum, without the potato!
This recipe uses one of my favorite vegetables - the kohlrabi!
A magical vegetable that tastes like very mild broccoli stalks and can act much like a potato. If you can't find kohlrabi, daikon radish will work as a sub, but the flavor will be slightly more radishy.

This is green kohlrabi (also comes in purple) so you know what you are looking for!

Recipe

- 2 lbs Daikon Radish or Green Kohlrabi* - peeled and sliced into approx 1/8 inch rounds
- 2 T Butter for pan
- 2 c Heavy Whipping Cream
- 1 tsp Salt
- Pepper to taste
- 1/2 c Gruyere Cheese
- 1/2 c Grated Parmesan
- Optional: 1/2 c thinly sliced Fennel or Leeks

Scalloped Fauxtatoes

Directions

- Preheat oven to 350, and butter a casserole dish.

- In a large pot, Pour cream, salt, and pepper and heat to a boil and immediately turn down to a simmer.

- Add fauxtato slices (and fennel/leeks, if using), and return to simmer to cook for about 5 minutes to start to soften fauxtatoes, and thicken the sauce.

- Pour (all) into the baking dish (try not to break up slices). and spread out evenly, with everything laying flat. Sprinkle the cheese over top. Cover with aluminum foil. Bake for 30 minutes.

- Remove foil, and bake another 15 minutes til nicely browned.

- Let sit for 10-15 minutes to cool slightly before serving.

Creamy Cauli-mash

Cauli-mash is a Keto staple, for good reason! It is fabulous on it's own or covered in gravy - keto-style, of course! If you tend to find cauli-mash a bit thin, follow the instructions here to thicken it up! Spending a bit of extra time is totally worth it!

Makes 8 servings.

Recipe

- About a 20-22 oz Cauliflower, cut into florets to make 16 oz usable parts
- 4 oz Cream Cheese
- 2 oz butter plus 2 T for topping
- Salt & Pepper

Directions

- Boil florets until very soft, about 5 minutes. Drain well.

- Immediately, while still hot, put in a food processor*, add the cream cheese and butter (except the 2 T for the top) generous pinch salt, and some pepper then blend until very smooth.

- If the texture is good for you, pour into bowl and top with 2 T butter. Serve!

- If you'd prefer a thicker mash, pour it into a pot and cook on medium heat, stirring and scraping the bottom regularly to avoid burning. You are trying to cook out some of the water. It should thicken over the next 10 minutes. When thicker, pour into the serving bowl and top with 2 T butter.

*You can also use a blender, but not one that seals completely, you can not put very hot items in those!

Velvety Celeriac Mash

What makes a mash as creamy, thick and rich as a potato but with 1/3 the carbs and a hint of delightful fresh celery flavor? CELERIAC!

The picture on this page was taken in a restaurant where I first had this delightful dish. They were kind enough to give me the recipe. They've since closed their doors, so I am sharing it with you! Celeriac (or celery root) is a bit higher carb than cauliflower, but still far less than a potato! The texture is remarkably similar to a potato and makes an incredible mash. There's a faint celery flavor like you seasoned your mashed potatoes with celery salt. Delightful.

Makes 8 servings.

Recipe

- 2 lbs Celeriac (celery root), peeled, cubed small (You'll need to buy closer to 3 lbs to net 2 lbs "meat")
- 1 cup bone broth + 2 cups water
- 1/4 c butter plus 2 T for topping
- 1 tsp kosher salt
- 1/4 tsp ground white pepper
- 1/4 cup whole milk or 2 T HWC plus 2 T Almond milk or similar

Velvety Celeriac Mash

Directions

- Peel and cube your Celeriac. The skin is thick and irregular (see picture), so I'd use a small knife rather than a peeler for skin removal.

- In a large pot, combine water and chicken broth/bone broth and bring to a boil, then add prepped Celeriac and boil until fork tender.

- Once ready, drain Celeriac and return to the pan off of the heat. Add milk, 1/4 cup butter, salt, and white pepper. puree in a food processor if it won't process, add more broth. If it's too thin after pureeing, put back in a cooking pot and cook out some of the water, scraping the bottom and stirring so it doesn't burn.

- Pour into a serving dish, make a little well in the center, and add 2 T of butter and sprinkle a pinch of salt over the top.

Neisha's Cornbread Dressing

A true holiday celebration side! Mixing the cornbready joy of Neisha's keto cornbread with her traditional southern dressing recipe!

Makes 8 servings.

Recipe

- Double Batch of Neisha's Cornbread
  - (see earlier recipe)*
- 1/2 c chopped Celery
- 1/4 c chopped Yellow Onion
- 2 hardboiled eggs, diced
- 1/2 c Butter, softened
- 1/2 c Chicken Bone Broth
- 1 T Dried Sage
- 1 tsp salt
- 1 tsp pepper

Directions

- After making Cornbread, let it cool and break it up into small pieces over a rimmed cookie sheet to expose the center. Leave out to dry out for several hours to overnight.

- 1-2 days later: Take the aforementioned cookie sheet filled with stale cornbread and place it in a 200-degree oven for 10 minutes to dry cornbread some more. Let cool. (if you missed the make cornbread early step, just start here)

- Put everything in a bowl (no, you don't need to precook the veggies) and mix well. It should form a sort of dough. Spread in a buttered casserole dish.

- Bake 350 for 40-45 minutes, until toasty on top! Let cool for 10-15 minutes, and serve!

Sweet Squash Puree

I know it looks like sweet potato, but it's actually Kabocha! The most common type of Kabocha is green. It's also sometimes called Japanese pumpkin. If you ever got pumpkin tempura in a Japanese restaurant, chances are good you've had Kabocha. The flesh inside is orange, even the green exterior. The skin is edible. You can slice and roast them with the skin on!

But if you want to make a puree, remove the skin for better texture.
Red Kabocha is sweeter than green, but both are pretty sweet - more like butternut squash than pumpkin.
Kabocha is flat on the bottom and has rough skin. That helps you distinguish it from similar such as Kori squashes (which are higher carb). Info on the carb count of Kabocha is a bit mixed, but general consensus is that it's in the same neighborhood as a pumpkin.

You'll want to cut it open and remove the seeds, then you can simply slice, rub with oil and salt and bake the slices and serve just like that or you can do as I did and turn the flesh into a puree!
If I want a thicker consistency like a puree, I always bake (you can also instant pot cook it whole) rather than cube a boil, as it absorbs water then - though that's great for soup preparations!

This is one of my favorite veggies.
Yes, more carbs than green leafies, but a lot less than starchier options like potatoes, and in the fall and winter can be a great comfort food.

INSIDE

Sweet Squash Puree

There seem to be two camps in the sweet potato world, load it up with sugar and toppings and make sweet potato casserole, or enjoy it in its (closer to) natural state, add some salt and butter, and call it good.

While I enjoy the novelty of the former, I am much happier with the latter. Especially since I tried Kobucha squash and realized how incredibly tasty they are on their own.

Makes 8 servings.

Recipe

- Two Kobucha squashes, about 12 lbs each (either green or red)
- 4 T butter
- Salt to taste

Directions

- Slice both Kabochas in half - if too hard to slice, pop them in the microwave whole for 2-3 minutes to soften slightly, then cut.

- Scrape out seeds and gunky strings attached to seeds and discard.

- Place cut sides down on a parchment-lined pan, and bake 350 for 40-60 minutes until internal flesh is very tender. If you don't think it's soft enough, cook longer.

- Scoop the flesh out from the skin, and discard the skin (it's edible but not puree texture).

- Add 4 T butter and Salt to taste. Serve! Yeah you can puree it in a food processor to get it even silkier if you want, but I've never seen the need - it's so smooth on its own.

Sweet Squash Casserole

You get me on the tastiness of the Kabocha, but you still want something more traditional with all the toppings. I got you! No problem.
When I first made this recipe years ago, I used a combo of cauliflower and pumpkin, but now that I am such a Kabocha fan, I see no reason to accept second best.

What would I do if I could not find Kabocha? I'd likely go for the butternut squash as it's naturally sweeter and doesn't require as much added sweetener to fool me it's sweet like the cauliflower did!

Recipe

- Puree from the previous recipe
- Toppings:
    - For Pecan Streusel:
        - 4 oz Pecans
        - 2 oz Salted Butter
        - 3 T Brown Sugar Swerve
    - For Marshmallow topping, let's be honest - I buy them.
        - Purchase: Max Mallow Burnt Caramel Marshmallows...
        - Make them with Allulose, water, gelatin, and vanilla - google "Keto Marshmallows"

Sweet Squash Casserole

Directions

- If you prepped Kabocha ahead and it's chilled, warm it to at least room temp before adding it to the dish.

- For one large casserole, put pureed Kabocha in the casserole dish. (Alternatively, you can make individual ones (as pictured) in small ramekins.)

For Pecan topping:
- Chop pecans, and mix with other ingredients. Sprinkle atop smoothed puree in the casserole dish.

- Bake 350 for 15 minutes, until pecans brown. Keep an eye on them to avoid burning!

- Serve!

- For marshmallow topping - DO NOT PUT KETO MARSHMALLOWS IN OVEN - they will become soup.

- Bake puree in a casserole dish for 15-20 minutes to allow it to get hot.

- Remove from oven and while still hot, top with marshmallows. They will get melty enough just from the heat.

- You can even go crazy and put marshmallows on top of the Pecan Streusel topping!

Green (not) Bean Casserole

Ah, Green Bean Casserole. So traditional, and yet... What? What's the issue you ask? Well, Dr. B is not the biggest fan of green beans in terms of their legume-ness.
So we created this recipe to replace the traditional green bean casserole!
We have to say we are super pleased. Actually obsessed with the fried onions. Those things are THE BOMB. And, let's be honest, aren't those the reason for the great love of this casserole?

Makes 12 servings as this dish is rich and filling.

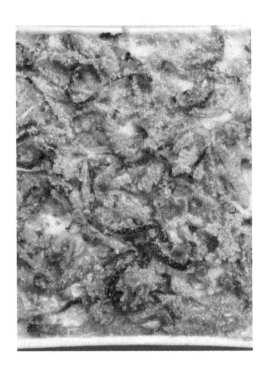

Recipe

- 1 lb Asparagus or Broccolini, tough ends removed and cut into 2" pieces
- 4 T Butter
- 15 Crimini (the brown kind) Mushrooms, sliced (white kind ok too!)
- 1 c Heavy Whipping Cream
- 2 Sprigs of fresh Thyme, leaves picked off stems
- 1/2 c Sour Cream
- 8 oz Grated Cheese Try Asiago or White Cheddar
- Salt and Pepper
- 1/4 c bone broth or chicken broth
- Optional: 4 strips of bacon, cooked and crumbled.

Fried Onion Topping:
- 1/4 large yellow onion sliced as thinly as possible
- 1/2 c heavy cream
- 2 c Pork Panko (crushed pork rinds)
- 1/2 c Grated Parmesan
- Enough olive oil to fill pan 1/4" deep
- 2 eggs, beaten

Green (not) Bean Casserole

Directions

- Preheat oven to 325°.

- Put onions in a bowl, and add cream and enough water to cover the onions. Let sit for an hour. Go about your business.

- After an hour passes, Drain the onions.

- Line a baking sheet with parchment and set it to the side.

- Take out three bowls (This might sound overcomplicated. But if you don't use the third bowl, your batter gets glunky from egg drops and you waste a ton. Trust me, it works best this way. If your batter gets glunky the batter won't stick.)
  - Put eggs in 1, and beat well.
  - Put panko and parm in another, and add a large spoon. (this is the breading)
  - Leave the third empty. I'll call this the action bowl.

- Follow this 5-step process to bread the onion:
  1. In the action bowl, lay down a scoop of the breading.
  2. Dip 6-8 pieces of the onion in the egg wash to coat well.
  3. Move them to the action bowl and place them on the breading layer.
  4. Top with a scoop of breading and press onto the onion.
  5. Carefully move to the baking sheet.

- Empty the action bowl of any remaining egg/batter mix.

- Repeat until all onion is breaded.

Green (not) Bean Casserole

Prep the casserole

- Boil water in a large pot, and add a generous pinch of salt. Parboil green veg for just 1-2 minutes. Drain and rinse with cold water to stop the cooking process. Set aside.

- In a deep frying pan, melt butter then cook mushrooms, seasoning with a pinch of salt and pepper, turn down the heat to medium, and add cream and thyme leaves.

- Cook down for 6-8 minutes to thicken, you want it steaming hot but never boiling. Remove from heat immediately and mix in sour cream and cheese (and bacon if using). Stir to combine and melt the cheese.

- Squeeze any remaining water out of green veg and place in an 8 x 11" baking dish. Pour sauce over top. Cover with aluminum foil. Place in oven and bake for 20 minutes.

- While that's baking, fry breaded onion that you've got waiting on a baking tray.
  - Put oil into the frying pan, doesn't need to be deep, just enough to fill the pan high enough that the onion will submerge. Heat medium-high.

  - When the oil is hot, add breaded onion one by one into oil to fry. Let sit for 1 minute then flip over to fry other side. Should only need 2-3 minutes to be completely cooked. Using a pair of kitchen tongs, move to a plate. (if oil gets too dirty, replace)

- When the casserole has baked for 20 minutes, remove from oven, remove foil, and top with fried onion. You'll likely have more than you need.

- Put back in the oven uncovered to toast up 10 more minutes

- Let sit 15 minutes before serving or someone will burn their tongue.

Cranberry Sauce

A staple at the holiday table. Homemade cranberry sauce requires very little change to make it keto - swap your sweetener and voila! But the type of sweetener matters... Erythritol will turn crispy and crunchy, and not in a good way.

You want to use allulose or xylitol for a true cranberry sauce experience. Unless you like the "who put sand in the cranberry?" experience.

Makes 8 servings.

Recipe

- Bag of Cranberries (around 12 oz)
- 1 cup water
- 1 Cup Allulose (less for more "tart")

- Optional: For Orange Cranberry Sauce:
- add 1/2 tsp Orange Extract and the zest of 1 orange.

Directions

- Put everything in a saucepan and bring it to a boil.

- Turn down to simmer for 10 minutes.

- Let cool. Transfer to bowl.

- Chill in the fridge for at least 3 hours. (If you messed up and didn't make this enough in advance to chill and finish gelling, separate it into smaller bowls to chill - it'll speed it up slightly)

Gravy

It's always a lot of fuss getting together gravy with fresh drippings, so if that stresses you out, simply make it with Tamari! Crazy but it totally works!

Makes 8 servings.

Recipe

- 2 C Stock (turkey or chicken)
- 2 oz butter
- 1/2 to 1 tsp Konjac Root powder
- If you have them: Pan Scrapings and fat drippings from Turkey
- if you do not have pan drippings: 2-4 tsp Tamari (wheat-free soy sauce) - it mimics the umami of pan drippings well!
- Pinch poultry seasoning

Directions

- In a saucepan, add stock and tamari or pan scrapings/drippings, if there are a lot of drippings, leave out all or some of the butter. Add spices. Taste - should be salty from drippings/tamari, but if bland, add some salt or additional tamari.

- Sprinkle 1/2 tsp konjac root over top and stir to combine completely. Cook for a few minutes to thicken more.

- If it's not thick enough, add 1/4 tsp more konjac at a time until thickened properly. Be aware it will thicken a bit more as it cools!

- Serve warm but not mouth-burningly hot.

Let's Talk Turkey

It's often expected at a holiday dinner... but so often it is dry and sad and only enjoyable covered in a shroud of gravy to hide its shame. But the bird can be delightful and moist. Here's the trick I learned listening to Nigella Lawson - who is a delightful cook... go watch one of her videos.

The trick to a perfect juicy turkey is...Cook, it upside down.

We all cook our turkeys breast up -and it looks great that way. But the white meat is on top through the whole roasting period... the part that cooks fastest and is the driest.

When you roast with the dark meat on top, while it cooks that lovely fat drips through the breast, making it far moister than it would be on its own. And if you don't overcook your turkey, the dark meat will still be plenty juicy! Ok ok, I'll admit it, the wings might be a bit singed. But it's a small sacrifice for the best turkey ever. (Can be mitigated by wrapping with a bit of aluminum foil on those.)

While your turkey looks a little less like a Butterball commercial when it comes out of the oven with this method, trust me it's a GAME CHANGER. (no not like the awful vegan movie. A real game changer.)

PRO TIP! Read the recipe all the way through before starting- or else you risk missing info and get it wrong!

Recipe

- A Turkey - Figure on 1 to 1.5 lbs per person
- Salt & Pepper
- Poultry Seasoning
- 1 Large Onion
- 2 Lemons
- Optional: Fresh herbs
- Required equipment: A good meat thermometer and pan to roast in (has sides)

Let's Talk Turkey

- First, never stuff a turkey with stuffing/dressing. One - it's an easy way to give people food poisoning. Two, the turkey isn't as good, mostly because by the time you've heated the internal temperature enough to not kill anyone, you have overcooked that turkey. (Some aromatics like herbs/lemons etc. are fine.)

- If you are good at planning ahead (I am not) have your turkey defrosted a day or two before you plan to cook it, and salt well, then store it in the fridge to "dry brine". It leads to a more flavorful and juicy bird.

- Day of: Double-check to make sure you removed all the giblets/neck/etc. from all the places. Let sit at room temperature for about 2 hours before cooking.

- Preheat oven to 425

- Rub turkey all over with a good deal of salt (if you dry brined, you already did this, so don't double up) and pepper and poultry seasoning. Cut your onion in half and stuff those pieces and the lemons in the cavity. If you have fresh herbs like thyme or rosemary add a few sprigs.

- Put turkey roasting pan BREAST SIDE DOWN. If you plan to eat the wings, cover them with a bit of foil. I use them for stock, so I don't bother. Put turkey in the oven and immediately turn it down to 350. DON'T FORGET TO TURN IT DOWN.

- Now you pretty much leave it alone for a while. It's self-basting due to its position.

- How long should it cook for? How long you cook a turkey is both a safety and taste issue. If you like your meat rubbery, dry, and tough, cook the breast to 170 degrees and you'll be happy. No one else will, but it's your turkey.

Let's Talk Turkey

- However, most of us like tender moist, and juicy birds, and we want to exercise a bit more care in finding the right equation. On the safety side, according to the USDA, Poultry is safe when it's reached 150 degrees and stayed there for a minimum of just under 4 minutes.

- Turkey eaters report happier eating with more cooked dark meat, and less cooked light meat. So even though technically safe at 150, the dark meat will be more pleasing a bit beyond that. Breast, however, begins to dry out much above that. This works perfectly with our cook upside-down plan, as the dark meat will receive more heat, and get to a higher temperature while protecting the light.

- The average cook time of a turkey to doneness is around 13 minutes per pound (at 350). But you want to go by temperature, not time. Therefore, I suggest checking it a bit earlier, so I say to follow this rule:

    - 12 minutes x # of pounds of Turkey = Time you should start checking the temperature. For example
        - 10 lb. turkey = 12 minutes x 10 = 120 minutes

- Check temp in both the thickest part of the thigh and the breast. If the temp is close, put it back in the oven and check every 10 minutes until you get there.
- Once your breast reaches 150 and the dark is a good deal above that (around 165) remove from the oven and let rest, tented with aluminum foil, for about 20 minutes. Then move to a cutting board and slice.

- The skin on the breast will be soggy and unappealing. I recommend discarding that rather than serving it. If you want to crisp that skin- after you rest the bird but before slicing, you can turn it breast side up and put it under the broiler for a few minutes and it should crisp up.

Cornish Game Hens

The Berry household traditionally serves this smaller bird instead of turkey!

8 servings

Recipe

- 4 Cornish game hens
- 3 tablespoons bacon fat
- salt and pepper to taste
- 1 lemon, quartered
- 8 sprigs of fresh rosemary, divided
- 24 cloves garlic
- ⅓ cup chicken bone broth

Directions

- Preheat the oven to 450 degrees. Rub hens with bacon fat; generously season with salt and pepper. Stuff 1 lemon quarter and 1 rosemary sprig into each cavity. Place hens in a large, heavy roasting pan and arrange garlic cloves around them.

- Roast in the preheated oven for 25 minutes. Meanwhile, whisk chicken broth, and 2 tablespoons of bacon fat together in a small bowl.

- Remove hens from the oven; reduce the oven temperature to 350 degrees. Pour liquid mixture over the hens and continue roasting, basting with pan juices every 10 minutes, until hens are golden brown and juices run clear about 25 more minutes. An instant-read thermometer inserted near the bone should read 165 degrees.

Cornish Game Hens

- Transfer hens to a platter, pouring any cavity juices into the roasting pan; discard lemons and rosemary. Tent hens with aluminum foil to keep warm.

- Transfer pan juices and garlic cloves to a medium saucepan; boil until reduced to a sauce consistency, about 6 minutes.

- Cut hens in half lengthwise and arrange two halves on each plate. Spoon sauce and roasted garlic on top. Garnish with remaining rosemary sprigs and serve.

Happy Hannukah

Ellen's Saucy Brisket

Texans will be confused about how sauced up this brisket is, but to Jews, stewed brisket is usually what we think when we hear brisket - not BBQ. Both are amazing and totally different, so no need to fight.

My mom celebrated Christmas at our house, but her sister, my Aunt Ellen did Hannukah at hers. I grew up a block from El's house, cutting through the backyard shortcut on my way to her house. Every year, El made this Brisket for Hannukah and it's a family favorite. This recipe was never written down, and delivered to me verbally, as most family traditions seem to be. As Ellen said, "The secret is to use an unreasonable amount of onions."

In case anyone is new to Jewish Traditions, there are many different sects of Judaism, some of which keep Kosher, some do not. My family is of the "not" variety so our meals can include dairy and meat in the same meal as you see here.

Recipe

- Large Brisket
- 4 Large Yellow Onions
- 4 Cloves Garlic
- 1 large Can of Diced Tomatoes
- 4 Large Bay Leaves
- Salt, Pepper, Onion Powder
- Smoked Paprika

Ellen's Saucy Brisket

Directions

- Heavily season your Brisket on all sides. Heat a large dutch oven to medium-high and put the fat side of the brisket down to render some fat into the pan and brown it. When the fat is nicely browned, brown the other sides of the brisket. Once done, remove the brisket to a plate. Using the rendered fat in the pan, add the onions and cook until browned. Add garlic and cook another 2-3 minutes. Put tomatoes into the pot, and stir with onions. Add Meat back in. Add enough beef stock to just cover the meat. Add bay leaves. Bring up to a simmer. Cover and cook for 4-5 hours. Checking now and again that it isn't burning.

- Let sit off the flame for 20 minutes or so, then remove the meat to the cutting board, and slice.

- Pour some of the sauce into gravy boats and serve with the meat.

Celeriac Latkes

You were introduced to Celeriac in the mash section, here it's being used for Latkes. Latkes are a traditional Hannukah food as it's fried in oil... and Hannukah is the celebration of oil!

On my YouTube channel, you can see I've done all the potato subs to come up with the tastiest latke, and Celeriac won hands down. Fry in Olive Oil, which is more traditional and, despite rumors to the contrary, can be a very healthy frying oil. But if you have Chicken Fat (Schmalz) that's also awesome - the smell of it frying is out of this world!

Makes 6 servings of 2 Latkes each.

Recipe

- About 2 lbs Celeriac to make 20 oz grated
- 2 eggs, beaten
- 2 oz Yellow Onion
- 1 tsp Salt
- generous sprinkle of onion and garlic powders
- Rendered Chicken Fat (Schmaltz) or Olive Oil for cooking (4-6 Tablespoons)
- Sour Cream and minced Chives for serving

Celeriac Latkes

Directions

- Peel and shred Celeriac and onion. Put both into a bowl and sprinkle with 1 tsp salt. Toss and let sit for 5-10 minutes. (salt will pull out moisture)

- Drain VERY WELL. Squeezing as much liquid as possible out with your hands. (Just sitting in the colander won't do it). The more water removed, the better they'll be!

- Add a generous sprinkle of onion and garlic powder. Toss. Now add in the egg a bit at a time to get the right texture. You don't want liquid swimming in the bowl. You might not need all the eggs. Just enough to hold it together.

- Heat a frying pan to medium-high, and add the fat. Once sizzling, form patties and cook a few minutes a side. Flip when ready. Make sure the spatula is under Latke well as they are a bit delicate until cooked.

- If a side seems undercooked, simply flip back and cook a bit more.

- Take care not to burn, lift the pan off the burner if you need to bring the temp down fast.

- Move Latkes to a paper towel-lined plate as they finish, and continue until all batter is used up.

- If you are doing multiple batches, heat the oven to warm and move latkes to a cookie sheet to sit in the oven on warm to stay warm while cooking the rest.
- If you have leftovers, put them on a cookie sheet in a 250-degree oven to reheat. You can reheat them in the microwave, but they'll be softer. The flavor will still be good!

- Serve topped with a dollop of sour cream or greek yogurt and a sprinkle of chives!

Zucchini Pancakes

While similar in appearance and pancake-fried deliciousness, they have a very different flavor than the Celeriac Latkes.

The fresh taste of zucchini and green onion plus the pungent note from parmesan give them an identity all their own.

Makes 6 servings

Recipe

- 1.5 lbs Zucchini
- 1 tsp Salt
- 4 Scallions, minced
- 1/3 cup Parmesan Cheese (grated)
- 1 egg, beaten
- pinch pepper, onion powder, and garlic powder (amount to taste)
- optional: 1/4 tsp coconut flour (will hold together a bit better when included)
- Olive Oil for frying

Zucchini Pancakes

Directions

- Shred Zucchini. Put into a bowl and sprinkle with 1 tsp salt. Toss and let sit for 5-10 minutes. (salt will pull out moisture)

- Drain VERY WELL. Squeezing as much liquid as possible out with your hands. (Just sitting in the colander won't do it). The more water removed, the better they'll be.
- Mix Zucchini with the rest of the ingredients except the oil.

- Heat a frying pan to medium-high, and add the oil. Once sizzling, form small patties with your hands and cook a few minutes a side. Flip when ready. Make sure the spatula is under Pancake well as they are a bit delicate until cooked.

- If a side seems undercooked, simply flip back and cook a bit more.

- Take care not to burn, lift the pan off the burner if you need to bring the temp down fast.

- Move Pancakes to a paper towel-lined plate as a finish, and continue until all batter is used up.

- If you are doing multiple batches, heat the oven to warm and move the pancakes to a cookie sheet to sit in the oven to stay warm while cooking the rest.

Sweet Kugel

Kugel is traditionally made with egg noodles (though can be made with potato or matzo too) and could be savory or sweet, though sweet is a bit more common, especially with noodles. And despite it being sweet, it's most definitely considered a side dish, served with the meal, rather than a dessert.

For those of you not familiar with Kugel, I'd describe it very much like bread pudding but made with egg noodles instead of bread. You might be surprised to see it here as a lower-carb option. I've subbed out the noodles for Spaghetti Squash, and while I'll admit it's not quite the same, it becomes something new and uniquely delish with the changes.

My Keto friend, Nancy Gordon, mentioned to me she uses sliced-up Egglife wraps as noodles - and I've done it. Works great! Just slice a pack of egglife tortillas into strips like noodles and replace the squash.

Recipe

- 16 oz cooked Spaghetti Squash - see method below
- 16 oz Cottage Cheese (I like Good Culture whole milk)
- 16 oz Sour Cream or full-fat Greek Yogurt
- 8 eggs, beaten
- 2 tsp Vanilla
- 1 tsp Cinnamon
- 1/4 to 1/2 cup Allulose
- few drops of Stevia Glycerite
- 4 Tablespoons butter, very soft, to grease the pan
- optional: 1 apple, peeled and grated (Can be omitted if adds too many carbs for you)
- optional unconventional ingredient: 1 scoop Snickerdoodle flavored Protein Powder such as PE science or Keto Chow. It gives it a firmer texture, but I love it added. Reduce sweetener, as the product is sweetened.

80

Sweet Kugel

Directions

- The only time-consuming part of this is cooking the spaghetti squash. I recommend doing that a day ahead so prep will be easy.

- When prepping the spaghetti squash, you want to do it in a method that dries it out as much as possible. Steaming it in an instant pot is great for other uses, but results in too wet a noodle, which makes the kugel soggy. For this I recommend cutting it into rings, scraping out the seeds, then laying the rings on a parchment-lined baking sheet. Do not add oil. Bake at 350 for 1 hour. Let sit until completely cool.

- The surface layer will form sort of a dryer film, scrape that off and discard, then using a fork, pull out the squash strings, discarding the peel. Place in a bowl and cover to store in the fridge until ready to assemble.

Making the Kugel:
- Generously butter a 9 x 13 casserole dish.

- In a large bowl, dump everything but the squash and beat to combine. No need to puree the cottage cheese or anything.

- Add squash and mix well to combine.

- Pour into baking pan. Bake at 350 until golden brown on the edges and set in the center, about 60-75 minutes.

- Let cool completely. Best served at room temperature.

- Feel free to chill in the fridge if making ahead, just leave out an hour or so before eating to bring the temp up a bit!

- This also makes a great breakfast (it's actually got a good amount of protein!) so I like to make extra!

Sweets & Drinks

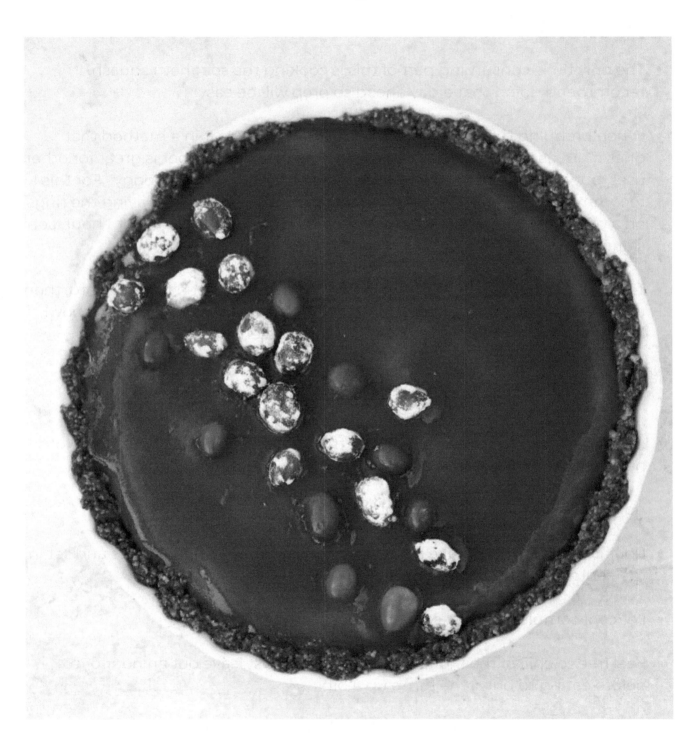

Jumble Cookies

This is a fun, easy cookie recipe.

Sort of like if granola was a cookie!

Makes about 10 cookies

Recipe

Part 1

- 1 egg
- 4 T Nut Butter (your choice)
- 2 T Butter, softened
- 1 tsp vanilla extract
- 2 T sweetener

Part 2

- 2 oz Chocolate or other similar chips
- 4-5 oz nuts, chopped
- 1-2 oz unsweetened coconut

Directions

- Prep a cookie sheet with parchment. Preheat oven to 350.

- Beat together Part 1 Ingredients until smooth.

- Put part 2 ingredients in a bowl and pour part 1 over, mix to combine, and shape into rounds.

- Place on parchment and bake for 15-18 minutes. Let cool on a sheet until room temperature.

Brown Butter Caramel Truffles

This recipe started as brown butter caramel for turtles (that recipe is on my YouTube) but I think it really shines turned into these truffles. These are a true indulgence!

Makes 10 balls

Recipe

- 1/2 c Salted Butter
- 1 cup Heavy Whipping Cream
- 1 cup chopped Pecans or Walnuts
- 2-3 T Brown Sugar Swerve
- 2 oz Cream Cheese
  - For topping:
  - Cocoa Powder & Cinnamon
  - Allulose and nut flour

Directions

- Heat butter in a medium saucepan on medium-high heat. You want to brown the butter, so let it cook and the butter solids on the bottom turn brown. You don't want them to get burned - if they end up looking like coffee grounds, they are burned. If that happens, throw it out and start again.

- Add sweetener and allow to dissolve, then add whipping cream. It will bubble up a bit. Simmer and allow to thicken. Let simmer until it looks glossy. There will be interesting patterns in it almost like a cartoon brain.

- Remove from heat and stir in Cream Cheese.

- Mix in chopped nuts.

- Scrape into a bowl and chill in the fridge for 2 hours. As they are butter based, do not leave them in a warm room for long!

Brown Butter Caramel Truffles

- I like to do a mix of coatings, but you can choose just one if you prefer! I would offer that the cocoa coating is much messier and tends to fall off a bit, so consider that with serving issues (and outfit choices!) Also, if cocoa melts into the butter a bit you'll get darker spots.

For Cocoa Cinnamon coating:
- 1/4 cup Unsweetened Cocoa
- 1 tsp Cinnamon
- 1 tsp Allulose

For Nutty coating:
- Blitz 1 oz nuts into flour, or use almond flour (if blitzing - don't overdo it, you want it powdery not wet)
- 2 tsp Allulose

- Take the mix out of the fridge, should be firm enough to scoop and shape.

- Spoon out with a teaspoon and roll in hand to shape into a ball.

- Roll in the topping of choice. Put it back in the fridge for at least an hour, but can be overnight, to continue to set.

Pumpkin Bread

One of Dr. Berry's favorite rare indulgences - especially with a hunk of salted butter on it!

Makes 12-14 slices

Recipe

- 8 Eggs - room temperature, separated
- 1/2 to 3/4 c Swerve Confectioners
- (depending how sweet you like!)
- 1.5 c Pumpkin Puree
- 2 T Coconut Oil or Butter
- 2 tsp Vanilla
- 3 oz Pork Panko (ground pork rinds)
- 3 T Coconut Flour
- 2 tsp Baking Powder
- 3 T Pumpkin Spice Mix
- optional topping: more PS mix and 2-3 T Pepitas

Directions

- Carefully separate your eggs.

- In a large bowl, mix all dry ingredients, making sure there are no obvious lumps. Then add everything but the egg WHITES. Beat until well-combined batter forms.

- Put the whites into a large bowl or stand mixer, beat eggs for a minute on low until frothy, then turn up to high until you have stiff peaks.

Pumpkin Bread

Directions

- Fold the whites into the other bowl, you want the whites completely integrated, but retain as much volume as possible.

- Line a bread pan with parchment paper. Pour in batter. Smooth top flat.

- If using, Sprinkle top with tsp Pumpkin Spice Mix and 2 T Pumpkin Seeds.

- Bake at 350 for 60-70 minutes, until a knife in the center comes out clean and there's no wetness. (If you want cupcakes, fill 12-15 silicone cupcake holders and bake 35ish mins instead)

- Let cool at room temperature and store in the fridge. This bread should be eaten at room temperature or warm, it's far better when not cold! So leave it on the counter a bit if it's been in the fridge.

- As I discovered by happy accident, if you put a slice in the microwave with a pat of butter on top and cook for x it turns into a sort of custard. Thank Dr. Ken Berry for this happy discovery.

- By the way, if you want this to be more of a "cake" just bake it in a cake pan! Cream cheese frosting is always a win!

Pumpkin Swirl Cloud Cake

This crust is based on cloud bread, so it's very fluffy. Topped with cream cheese and pumpkin - it's a mash-up of pumpkin cheesecake, cloud bread, and breakfast danishes!

Recipe

CHEESECAKE LAYER

- 8 oz Cream Cheese, softened
- 1/2 tsp Vanilla Extract
- 3-4 drops of Stevia Glycerite
- 1 egg

PUMPKIN LAYER

- 8 oz Pumpkin Puree
- 3-4 drops of Stevia Glycerite
- 1 T Allulose
- 2 T Brown Sugar Swerve (or similar)
- 15 grams Keto Chow Pumpkin Spice Caramel (or similar)
- 1 tsp Pumpkin Pie Spice Mix *
- 1 T Heavy Whipping Cream
- 2 Egg Yolks

CLOUD BREAD CRUST
PART A

- 4 Egg Yolks
- 15 grams of unflavored Whey Protein
- 15 grams Keto Chow Pumpkin Spice Caramel (or similar)
- 1-2 T Sweetener (or similar)
- 2 oz Sour Cream

:PART B

- 6 egg whites
- Pinch Cream of Tartar

Pumpkin Swirl Cloud Cake

Directions

- You'll need 4 bowls!

- Put all the ingredients for the cheesecake in one bowl, and beat until creamy and smooth.
- Put all the ingredients for the Pumpkin layer in another, and beat until creamy and smooth.
- Put Part A of the crust in a third bowl (should be a big one!) then beat until smooth and runny.
- Put Part B into a mixer bowl and beat to STIFF peaks using either a stand mixer or a handheld electric mixer. Do not under beat them!
- Mix one scoop of B into A, then fold in until uniform but still as poofy as possible!
- The perfect size pan is a jelly roll pan (10 x 15") but a 9 x 13" will do too. Line with parchment and very lightly spray with oil then run hands over to distribute. It should be a tiny amount, sort of like you're moisturizing the parchment. Too much and it'll be soggy.
- Spread crust on parchment, leaving a raised edge. Then spread on the cream cheese layer, then the pumpkin, and swirl with a fork- just the cream cheese and pumpkin layers, so don't push down all the way through with a fork.

- Bake 325 for 22-25 minutes. Do not overbake. You want the center with a bit of wobble but not liquidy at all.

- Cool completely before slicing. Cut carefully to avoid tearing the pastry

Sour Cream Pecan Coffee Cake

Many folks seem confused about coffee cake, thinking it should have coffee in it. Nope! It's a cake you'd serve with coffee!
This cake is very dense, not a "light fluffy" one.

Makes 9 large or 12 smaller slices

Recipe

CAKE LAYER

- 8 T Butter (use salted)
- 1/2 c swerve confectioner's
- 2 eggs
- 1 c fine almond flour
- 5 T coconut flour
- 3 T sour cream
- 2 tsp vanilla extract
- 1 T Baking Powder
- 1/4 tsp Xanthan gum
- 1/3 cup Almond (or other unsweetened nuts) Milk - plus more if needed

CREAM CHEESE LAYER

- Cream Cheese layer
- 4 oz cream cheese
- 1 egg
- 2 T Sweetener
- 1/2 tsp vanilla

TOPPING

- 4 oz Pecans
- 2-3 T Swerve Brown Sugar (or similar)
- 1.5 tsp cinnamon
- 2 T butter (salted)

Sour Cream Pecan Coffee Cake

Directions

- Make the Cake Layer:
- In a smaller bowl, mix almond flour, coconut flour, baking powder, and xanthan gum - breaking up lumps with a fork.

- In a larger bowl, cream together butter and sweetener, and add 1 egg at a time, beating until incorporated before adding a second. Then add sour cream, almond milk, and vanilla. Beat until smooth.
- Beat dry mixture into egg mix slowly in batches. Beating between each batch. Add more almond milk if the batter seems too dry. Set aside.

- Cream Cheese Layer: In a separate bowl beat together all ingredients listed. Set aside.

- Chop pecans fairly small. Some mediums are fine, but you want mostly minis. Put in a new bowl with swerve and cinnamon. Mix. Then melt butter and pour over. Mix.

Assemble:
- Grease a 8 x 8 or so brownie pan or similar. (will work in a pie pan)
- Add cake mix and smooth flat.
- Cover evenly with a cream layer.
- Cover with a nut layer. Press in but don't submerge nuts.
- Bake 350 for 33-38 min
- Let cool completely before slicing.
- If want sharper edges, once cool, place in the fridge for at least 2 hours, then slice while chilled.
- The flavor is best at room temperature, so take it from the fridge in advance of serving.

Tiramisu

A traditional Italian Dish, Keto-fied! I made this for Ken Berry's birthday a few years back, and it's on his short list of special occasion treats! The cake took a while to dial in, and while it's not required adding the Keto Chow Caramel Macchiato makes that cake AMAZING. Well worth the additional purchase.

While it takes a while to make, it's make ahead, so that's convenient for a party!

Makes 12 servings.

Recipe

- ○ Custard:
- 4 egg yolks (reserve whites for cake)
- 1/4 c Allulose
- 2 tsp vanilla (can also use rum)
- 1/4 c heavy cream
- 1/4 c almond milk (or other nut milk)
- ½ tsp gelatin (optional)

- ○ Cake:
- 3 whole eggs, separated
- Reserved egg whites from custard
- Pinch cream of tartar
- 4 T Allulose
- 1 c fine almond flour
- 1 T + 1 tsp Coconut Flour OR 4 T Keto Chow Caramel Macchiato or vanilla flavor (highly recommend the Caramel Macchiato!)
- 1 tsp vanilla
- 1 tsp baking powder

- ○ Espresso Soak:
- 4 Shots of Espresso (can also use cold brew)
- 3-4 drops Stevia Glycerite or 1 T Allulose
- 2 T rum or 1 tsp rum extract

- ○ Cream:
- 2 c heavy whipping cream
- 8 oz mascarpone, room temperature
- 3-4 drops Stevia Glycerite or 3-4 drops Lakanto Vanilla Monk FruitDrops
- (the custard made in step 1)

- For Garnish and layers:
- Unsweetened Cocoa Powder
- Optional: Keto Friendly Dark Chocolate

Tiramisu

Directions

Step 1: Make the Custard. (This step takes about 10 minutes of effort)

- Prepare a double boiler by choosing a bowl that will fit over a pot without falling in. Put a few inches of water in the pot and begin to bring it to a boil. Do not put the bowl on yet as we want it to start cool.

- In that set-aside bowl, pour cream in and sprinkle gelatin over the surface to bloom.

- Let cream/gelatin sit for 3-5 mins. while the water boils, then move over steam and mix well to incorporate the gelatin completely.

- When smooth, quickly add the yolks with sweetener and vanilla and whisk constantly so it doesn't "scramble" the eggs.

- Cook slowly, stirring constantly so it cooks but doesn't burn or scramble.

- Keep cooking until it thickens significantly. This takes longer than you think it should. Slow is safer than fast! No one likes to waste cream and eggs.

- Remove from heat and let cool to room temperature, then beat with room temperature Mascarpone. (Always combine similar temperatures or you'll run into clumping)

Tiramisu

Directions

Step 2: Make the cake. A jelly roll pan (10 x 15" is perfect, but if you only have a 9 x 13" that's ok, but don't snack on the cake until you are sure you have enough to cover! It'll be tight :)

- Measure out almond flour, and add other dry ingredients to the flour, mixing to combine. Set aside.

- Pour whites into a mixing bowl and add whole eggs. Sprinkle with cream of tartar. (No we aren't making meringue, so adding yolks works, we are just making very fluffy eggs). Beat on high until tripled in volume, about 5-6 minutes.

- Mix in vanilla. Sprinkle the dry ingredients over the wet and fold them in. Preserving as much fluffiness as possible, but getting the flour mix fully distributed.
- Cover the pan with parchment paper and spread the batter evenly.

- Bake at 350, 10-15 minutes until well browned.

- Cut the cake into pieces about the size of 2 fingers together. You'll be arranging them in two layers in the finished dish. It's ok if there are small gaps.

Step 3: Make the Cream.

- Beat the Heavy Whipping Cream with sweetener to soft peaks. Beat on medium - don't break the cream. Treat it gently.

- Fold in the Custard/Mascarpone until smooth.

94

Tiramisu

Directions

Step 4: Make the Soaking liquid & Assemble:

- Mix all soaking ingredients. The amount of rum is dependent on how boozy you like it! (Adjust to suit taste)

Assembly:
- Pour 1/2 c unsweetened cocoa into a measuring cup and have a dry fine sieve at the ready.

- Pour the soaking liquid into a shallow dish, and dip cake fingers one flat side down into the liquid, you only want liquid about halfway through - DO NOT fully saturate. It'll make everything too soggy. Lay soak side up into an 8x8 pan. Continue until the layer is complete. You do not need them crowded together, almost touching is good.

- Top with about half the mascarpone/custard/cream mix.

- Using a sieve, shake a layer of cocoa over the cream layer. You want it fairly covered as the cocoa adds a nice flavor.

- Add the second cake layer using the same soak method as before. Top with remaining cream.

- Using a sieve sprinkle the remaining cocoa over the top in a finer layer- you'll see this layer, so go a little lighter and prettier!

- *Optional addition: Finely chop the Keto-friendly dark chocolate and sprinkle over the top.
- Move to the fridge to set and chill at least 2 hours before serving, but overnight is best.

Southern Chocolate Pie

Just like Neisha's Grandma used to make!
Chocolatey and not too sweet!
If you are intimidated by meringue, you can
always top it with whipped cream instead.

Makes 12 servings

Recipe

Crust
- 7 oz almond flour (weigh it, what
  this is in cups is super variable)
- 4 T Butter, cut into small pieces
  and very cold
- pinch salt
- 1 tsp Swerve Confectioners
- 1 egg white (reserve yolk for filling)

Filling
- 1/2 c plus 2 T unsweetened Cocoa
- 1/3 c Swerve Confectioners Sweetener
- 1 tsp vanilla extract
- 4 egg yolks + 1 whole egg
- 1 and 2/3 c heavy whipping cream
- 1/2 tsp coconut flour

Meringue
- 6 Egg Whites (no bit of yolk can be present!)
- 1/2 tsp cream of tartar
- 2 T Allulose

Southern Chocolate Pie

Directions

Make the Crust:

- Mix the crust ingredients. Smoosh in butter so you've formed a ball of dough that still contains some whole butter pieces.

- Roll out flat and lay over the pie pan and press into shape.

- Cut off the edges of the crust so it's flat to the top of the pie pan vertically. It should not be extended over the edge at all. You're going to completely hide the crust with a meringue layer, so the edge doesn't burn.

- Bake in a 350 oven for 15 minutes, until the bottom is browned a bit. Set aside to cool.

Make the Custard:

- In a pot, beat together everything but the vanilla. Begin heating on medium-high, and stirring constantly cook for 5 minutes or so, until thickened and bubbling slightly. Turn off the heat, add vanilla, and continue to stir for another 2-3 minutes.
- Pour into prepared pie crust.

You'll want to do the next step right away as it's best to top custard while still hot.

Southern Chocolate Pie

Directions

Make the Meringue:

- Put whites in a mixer bowl and beat on medium until frothy. Sprinkle cream of tartar over the top, turn on low then turn up to high and beat until begins to turn white. Turn down to low and add sweetener, and beat in and return to high to beat until truly stiff peaks form. This is when you lift the beater straight up, a peak forms that points up and doesn't fall over. This is the trick to high meringue!

(There's a great video on Martha Stewart's website just google "Martha Stewart Whipping Egg Whites")

  - Meringue failure is almost always due to under-beating.

  - Yes, you can also over-beat it. You don't want it to be chunky! stop before it starts breaking up. As soon as stiff peaks will form, stop.

- Carefully top hot Custard (already in the crust) with Meringue.

- Form into a domed shape, careful not to mix the custard layer with egg whites. Using a teaspoon, create shapes and peaks on top of the meringue to create a design. High points will brown in the oven, and depressions will stay white.

- Bake at 350 for 15 minutes.

- Remove from oven, cool to room temperature, then move to the fridge to chill for 3-4 hours. Best served the day of to avoid meringue falling and weeping. (Yes, that's as sad as it sounds.)

Cranberry Cream Pie

I created a cranberry gelee topping for this pie to get the shiny cranberry color appearance. This is optional. I created it because the pie filling is more pink than garnet (see cut pie photo above), which wasn't the look I was going for. However, it's delicious without fussing with the topping. You can also cover it with whipped cream and dot it with cranberries! It is YOUR pie, honey, you do you!

I've versions with and without the top layer below.

I like things pretty darn tart, so I've suggested a range of sweetener level so you can make it work for your tastes.

This is a flavor sensation. Plan on it being 10 servings.

Recipe

Filling

- 12oz Cranberries (previously frozen is fine!) (set aside 12-18 for decorating)
- 3 eggs+3 egg yolks
- 1 tsp Lemon Zest
- 1 tsp Lime Zest
- pinch salt
- 3/4 c unsalted butter, softened
- 1/2 to 1 c Allulose (to taste)
- 1/2 c water

99

Cranberry Cream Pie

Gelee Topping
- 6 oz Cranberries
- 1/4 c water +1 T
- 1 T Lime Juice (1/2 a lime)
- 1 tsp gelatin
- 3 -4 T Confectioner's Swerve
- 3-4 drops Stevia Glycerite

Optional:
- A few reserved cranberries
- Sweetener, powdered
- 1 c Heavy Whipping Cream to whip for serving

Crust
- 6 oz Pecans
- 5 oz Ginger Cookies or similar - use either Fat Snax or a recipe that follows
- 2 oz Butter
- 2-4 T Swerve Brown Sugar

Directions

- Make the crust. Pulse nuts and cookie pieces in a food processor to fine crumbs. Pick out and reprocess any bigger chunks.

- Add butter and Swerve. Mix.

- Take out a 9" pie pan. Butter pan and turn mix into the pan. With clean wet hands, press the crust into the pan evenly. Let come up the sides and press into place. The edges won't be a smooth fine edge, but that's fine. If the crumbs start to stick to your hands, rinse. Clean hands work, sticky hands don't.

- Cook 350 for 12-14 minutes, until lightly browned but not burned! Set aside.

Cranberry Cream Pie

Directions

- Make the filling: Put clean cranberries in a pot with 1/2 c water and 1/2 c sweetener, bring to a boil, and then turn down to simmer for 10-12 minutes, stirring occasionally. Cranberries are done when most of the liquid is cooked out and almost all the berries have burst and you have thick cranberry jam.

- Let cool for a few minutes then when warm instead of hot, pour into a food processor or strong blender and puree until smooth. Add a few tablespoons of water if the puree won't blend. Taste the puree, if not sweet enough add a bit more sweetener.

- Set up a double boiler and make sure the bowl won't be touching the boiling water.

- Into a cold bowl, scrape in the remaining puree, and add eggs, yolks, zests, pinch salt, and lime juice.

- Beat and place over the boiling water. Using a scraper, continuously mix and scrape the bottom and sides of the bowl. Cook for about 10 minutes, until becomes thick. Remove from heat for 15 minutes to cool.

- Scrape into the mixer bowl (stand or bowl with electric beaters). Begin beating on medium adding a tablespoon at a time of the butter into the bowl, beating well between each addition (or with the stand mixer continually running). Continue until all butter is completely incorporated. Beat another 2-3 minutes to fluff.

- Pour/scrape filling into cooled pie crust. If you are planning glossy topping, make sure the filling is flat. If not, swirl the top. Move to fridge to chill.

Cranberry Cream Pie

Directions

If making Gelee Topping:
- In a side bowl, add 1 T water and 1 T lime juice. Sprinkle top with gelatin. Let sit while making cranberry.

- Put cranberries in a pot with 1/4 c water and 1/4 c sweetener. Bring to a boil. Simmer for 8-10 minutes. Watch closely the last 5 minutes, scraping the bottom regularly because burning is a risk! Add bloomed gelatin and stir to incorporate. When very thick and jelly-like, remove from heat and push through a fine mesh sieve into a clean saucepan.

- Pour into a pitcher or measuring cup with a spout and let cool to room temperature.

- Take the pie out of the fridge and carefully pour the topping over the pie to create a glossy cranberry layer, slightly tilting the pie to distribute.

- Return to the fridge to continue chilling.

- Chill for AT LEAST 4 hours. (too little chilling = not set filling)

Optional decoration -
Parboil reserved cranberries and roll some in powdered sweetener.
Lay out on top of the pie as desired. I leave some plain, and some powdered. Sprinkle a bit of lime zest if desired as well.

Or just plop on some whipped cream and call it yum!

No'Nana Pudding

ITraditional Banana Pudding uses layers of cut banana, we skip that to save the carbs adding some banana extract instead. If not a fan of banana, you can make a cranberry version by using vanilla extract instead of banana and adding a spoonful of cranberry sauce in between one of the layers!

Makes 4 servings

Recipe

- 3 egg yolks
- 2-3 T Allulose
- 4-5 drops of Stevia Glycerite
- 2 c Heavy Whipping Cream
- 1/2 tsp Vanilla Extract
- 3/4 tsp Banana Flavoring
- 4 oz Cookie Crumbs (see the following page)

- Note: If you want to use a boxed pudding mix instead of making it from scratch, while not optimal, Simply Delish brand is much more Keto friendly than any other store-bought option! They make a banana and a vanilla one.

Directions

To make the pudding:

- In a saucepan, combine yolks, 1 cup of cream, sweeteners, and extracts.

- Beat well, then turn the heat on to medium. Cook, whisking constantly. The mixture should never boil, if seems too hot remove it from the heat. Cook until thickens to pudding consistency. Remove from heat. Cool to room temperature.

- Take out a bowl and beat the remaining cup of cream to soft peaks. Set aside about 1/4 cup, and fold the rest into the cooled pudding.

- Assemble: In 1 large serving bowl, or 4 small ones.
  - Take cookie crumbs and distribute about 2 oz as the bottom layer.
  - Top with 1/2 the pudding, and repeat with cookie crumbs, reserving a bit to sprinkle as a topping. Put the final layer of pudding and a dollop of reserved pure whipped cream on top (if you forgot to set it aside not a problem)
  - Sprinkle remaining cookie crumbs on top.

- Set in fridge for 1 hour before serving.

Directions:

Ginger Cookies for Crumbs

IIf you need a time saver, High Key makes a good ginger spice cookie that could work great!

Recipe

Dry Ingredients
- 2 c Almond Flour (fine)
- 1/4 c Swerve Brown Sugar
- 2 tsp ground ginger
- small pinch nutmeg
- small pinch cloves
- pinch salt
- 1/2 tsp ground cinnamon
- 1 tsp baking soda

Wet Ingredients
- 1 egg
- 4 T butter, very soft
- 1 tsp vanilla

- Take out two bowls and put wet ingredients in one, and dry in the other.

- Mix dry ingredients so well incorporated.

- Beat together wet ingredients and begin to incorporate dry by adding in several parts, beating between each addition until completely combined.

- Prep a cookie sheet with parchment.

- Take a tablespoon of cookie dough and with clean, damp hands, roll it into a ball and place it on parchment. Continue until all rolled.

- Flatten with flat fingers. The thinner the cookie, the crispier.

- If there is more than fit on your sheet, can do it in 2 batches.

- Bake for 9-11 minutes. Let cool on a sheet until room temperature.

- To make crumbs, break them up with your fingers.

German Chocolate Cake

German is the name of the creator, not the country of origin. This is an American invention!

Makes 8-12 slices (it's rich!)

Recipe

Cake
- 2 oz. unsweetened baking chocolate
- 1/2 cup unsalted butter
- 5 large egg(s)
- 2 Tbsp. cocoa powder
- 1/2 cup fine almond flour
- 50 grams Chocolate Keto Chow or similar*
- 1 Tbsp. coconut flour
- 1/2 tsp. baking soda
- 1 tsp. baking powder
- 1/2 cup Allulose
- 1 Tbsp. pure vanilla extract
- 1/2 cup heavy cream

Protein Powders - in all my baking I use either Keto Chow or another combination of Whey and Casein such as PE Science. This combination of protein types has the best outcome in baked goods. Keto Chow adds salt, but if I use PE Science, I add a pinch.

Filling
- 1 cup raw pecan unsalted
- 1 cup unsweetened coconut flakes
- 6 oz. heavy cream
- 3 large egg yolk
- 1/2 cup unsalted butter melted
- 1/2 cup brown erythritol blend
- 1 tsp. pure vanilla extract

Decoration
- 10 whole raw pecans set aside for decoration
- 2 Tbsp. unsweetened coconut flakes, loosely chopped, set aside for decoration

Directions

- Preheat the oven to 325°F. Once preheated, spread one cup of pecans on a rimmed baking sheet and roast for eight minutes. Add 1 cup of coconut flakes and cook an additional 2 minutes until the coconut gets a little toasted. Allow to cool then chop into smallish pieces.

German Chocolate Cake

- In a medium saucepan on medium heat, whisk together the cream, egg yolks, butter, sweetener, and vanilla, whisking constantly so it doesn't burn. Cook for about 5-8 minutes, or until it begins to thicken. It's done when it's reached the thickness of condensed milk. Pour into a bowl to cool to room temperature.

- Stir nuts & coconut into the thickened mixture.

- Meanwhile, prepare the cake. Butter the sides and bottom of two 8" cake pans, then line the bottom of each pan with parchment paper.

- Mix all the dry cake ingredients in a large bowl, then set aside.

- Chop the chocolate small, and place it in a bowl along with the butter. Microwave just long enough to melt, don't let it burn. Stir. Set aside to cool slightly.

- Using a stand mixer or electric mixer, beat the eggs on low until frothy. Then increase speed to high and beat for about 5 minutes, or until light in color and about tripled in volume.

- Pour the cooled melted chocolate/butter mixture, as well as the vanilla and heavy cream, into the eggs and beat until combined.

- Fold in the dry ingredients gently. The mixture will lose some air.

- Pour half into each pan and bake on the center rack at 325°F for 28-32 minutes, or until they are bouncy to the touch, and a knife comes out of them clean. Let cool completely, completely (if warm, topping will drip), and remove the pan.

- Put one cake on a serving plate and top it with half of the filling. Repeat with the second cake and topping. Decorate with pecans and coconut.

- Store any leftover cake in the fridge, but bring it to room temperature to serve.

Chocolate Mint Mousse Pie

I hear some people aren't fans of chocolate with mint. It's a crazy world we live in! Mint + chocolate is such a winter treat!

Makes 8 servings.

Recipe

Crust
- 1 cup fine almond flour
- 2 tbsp fine almond flour
- 1/4 to 1/2 cup Allulose
- 1/3 cup cocoa powder
- 1 egg beaten
- pinch salt
- 3 tbsp salted butter melted, plus more for greasing the pan

Filling
- 16 oz cream cheese softened
- 1/2 cup powdered sweetener swerve
- 2 cups heavy cream
- 100 g Chocolate Mint Keto Chow or similar
- 1/2 tsp mint extract
- 1/2 tsp vanilla extract
- Optional: 5-8 drops of green food coloring

Directions

- Preheat oven to 350F. Grease a 9-inch pie pan and set aside.

- Mix together dry ingredients for the crust, then add the butter to the egg, then pour into the dry ingredients. Using your hands, mix wet and dry ingredients together to form a dough. Remove 4 tbsp worth of dough and set aside.

Chocolate Mint Mousse Pie

Directions

- Take the remaining dough and roll it into a ball, then flatten it into a disk, and put it in your prepared pie pan. With wet hands (it helps!), smooth and press the dough into the pie pan to form a pie crust. Prick holes in the base of the crust using a fork.

- Take a baking sheet and put a bit of parchment on it. Take the reserved dough and flatten it into a pancake (you're crumbling it, so it doesn't have to be pretty) on the parchment paper

- Put both pie and baking sheet into the oven, if it can fit. You can also do the baking in two stages if needed. Bake for 12-14 minutes. Set aside to cool completely.

- Take a pancake piece and crumble it into what looks like cookie crumbs.

- Now prepare your filling. Beat your softened cream cheese for 2-3 minutes, then add sweetener, extracts, Keto Chow, 3/4 cup of the cream, and the food coloring (if using). Beat until smooth and fluffy.

- In a clean bowl, beat the remaining cream to soft peaks. Set aside about 1/2 cup for topping. Fold half the whipped cream into the mint mixture.

- Scoop mint mousse into the cooled pie shell. Top with whipped cream. Smooth into a dome shape.

- Top with crumbled crumbs.

- Chill for 4 hours or overnight.

Eggnog

Can be made with or without booze! If preparing for a mixed crowd, omit booze and add to drinks individually instead!

Makes 8 servings.

Recipe

- 2 cups unsweetened nut milk (like cashew, almond, or macadamia nut...)
- 2 c Heavy Whipping Cream
- 1/4 to 1/2 c Allulose
- 6 large egg yolks
- 1/4 cup bourbon, (optional)
- 1/4 c dark rum (optional)
- Freshly grated nutmeg (optional)

Directions

- In a saucepan, mix cream, "milk" and sweetener and heat.

- In another bowl, beat yolks and slowly pour the hot cream mixture into the yolks, whisking vigorously so they warm without cooking. Then pour the mixture back into the pan and cook over low heat stirring regularly until thickens (do not boil), about 15 minutes (cook longer to thicken even more, if you want thinner, add more "milk"/cook less time).

- Your signal is it's thickened enough: Should coat the back of a spoon. Strain into pitcher (or punch bowl) and stir in bourbon and rum (feel free to adjust the quantity or only use one based on your tastes), if using.

- Let cool completely and put in the fridge for at least an hour to chill. Grate fresh nutmeg over top.

Coquito (Puerto Rican Nog)

Eggnog with a Cuban Twist!

8 servings.

Recipe

- 1 c unsweetened Cashew, almond, or other nut milk
- 15 oz can of Coconut Milk
- 1.5 c Heavy Whipping Cream
- 2 egg yolks
- Pinch Cinnamon
- Pinch Nutmeg plus Freshly grated Nutmeg for topping
- 4 - 8 T Allulose
- 1/2 tsp Vanilla Extract
- Optional: 4-8 oz White Rum

Directions

- In a saucepan, mix cream, milk, and sweetener and heat.

- In another bowl, beat yolks and slowly pour the hot cream mixture into the yolks, whisking vigorously so they warm without cooking. Then pour the mixture back into the pan and cook over low heat until thickened, about 5 minutes.
- Add vanilla, pinch nutmeg and cinnamon, and rum (if using) and pour into a blender and blend until frothy.

- Pour into a pitcher and chill until cold. Before serving, top with nutmeg.

- Let cool completely and put in the fridge for at least an hour to chill. Grate fresh nutmeg over top.

Hot Cocoa 2 ways

Nothing is quite as comforting as a good cup of cocoa! Here are two flavor variations.

2 servings.

Recipe

- 3 c unsweetened Cashew, almond, or other nut milk
- 1/2 c Heavy Whipping Cream
- 1/4 c Unsweetened Cocoa Powder
- 4 - 8 T Allulose
- 1/2 tsp Vanilla

Optional additions:
- For Mexican:
  - 1/4 tsp cinnamon
  - 1/8 tsp cayenne
- For Mint:
  - 1/8 tsp Mint Extract
- For both:
- Whipped cream and shaved chocolate

Directions

- In a saucepan, combine all ingredients, and simmer low for 5-8 minutes.

- Pour into 2 mugs, top with whipped cream, and sprinkle with shaved chocolate - or if you have some Keto-friendly marshmallows (Max Mallow brand makes several flavors!) you can top with those.

Pumpkin Spice Latte

Makes one latte, but feel free to multiply ingredients and prep in advance, omitting coffee until serving and combining then!

Recipe

- 12 oz Coffee
- 1-2 T Pumpkin Puree (can omit if don't have)
- 1/2 to 1 tsp Pumpkin Spice Mix
  - (plus a pinch for the top)
- 1/4 c Heavy Whipping Cream
- 1/2 c Unsweetened Almond Milk
- 6 drops Pumpkin Pie Spice Stevia
- 1/2 to 2 tsp Granulated Sweetener
- 1/4 c Heavy Whipping Cream, whipped for top

Directions

- Combine the smaller quantities of all the ingredients, not yet adding whipped cream topping in a blender or a cup with a frother. Taste.

- Add more pumpkin, spices, or sweeteners to suit your tastes.

- Top with Whipped Cream and pinch spice.

Made in the USA
Las Vegas, NV
20 November 2023

81252453R00063